How to Open An Adoption:

A guide for parents
and birthparents
of minors

Patricia Martinez Dorner

ISBN 0-9641035-8-3
© by Patricia Martinez Doerner
First printing 1998
Printed in the United States of Amer

R-Squared Press, 721 Hawthorne, Royal Oak 48067
Phone and FAX: (248) 543-0997

Dedication

I would like to dedicate this book to Ernie Santos, whom we had the joy of knowing for eleven years before his untimely death in November 1997. The brother of my daughter, Jennifer, the brother in spirit of my other daughter, Katherine, he will be remembered for his loving spirit. We, who are left behind, are grateful that through the opening of our adoption we were joined as family.

I thank Gloria Guzman, his mother, Jennifer's birthmother and Katherine's "other mother," for having the courage to face her emotions in opening the door to contact.

I also dedicate this book to my daughters, Jennifer and Katherine, who have guided my understanding and are the center of my life.

Acknowledgments

I would like to thank all the people who taught me how important life relationships are. At the top of the list are my parent, Susan and Joseph L. Martinez.

I would like to express my grateful appreciation to all those families, both birthfamilies and adoptive families, who have entrusted the opening of their adoptions to me. Each time a reconnection happened, it reinforced my conviction that this is a sound practice, even will all the complexities. Special thanks to the children and youth who shared their personal journeys with me. Special thanks also to Lexie, Adam, Aaron, Casey, Joy, and Jewel for allowing me to share their letters with others.

Thanks to Mary Martin Mason, Marcy Axness, and Martha Weiss for spending time and energy giving me feedback on the work in progress. I know how much time and effort it takes to do this.

Thanks to Kathleen Silber and Phyllis Speedlin, co-authors of *Dear Birthmother*, and to David Bowen and Joe Labatt of Corona Publishing for allowing me to cite the four myths of adoption.

Thanks to Diana Rowe for thoughtfully endorsing the practice of open adoption by sharing the effects on her family.

Contents

Preface

Letters from Adopted Children

First letter from Jewel; age 15 when contact was established with her birthmother, Erin.

Dear Erin,
Some people would say that a puzzle can never be finished even if only one piece is lost. And it's been a very important and sacred wish for me to finally discover my missing link (my puzzle piece), in order to make my picture complete.

I feel no anger towards this piece, only anticipation and longing for the day when I can be at peace with myself.

I really have no clue where to begin. I am so nervous because I thought I'd never, even in my wildest dreams, imagine that I would see the day when I could actually come this close to communicating with the woman who allowed me to be brought into this world.

I suppose it would be easiest to start with my name, it's Jewel. I'm 15 years old and that would probably make you about 34 or 35 now, huh? (Are you feeling OLD yet?) I'm about 5'7" and have short blond hair and hazel eyes. And presently I am living in Delaware (Dela-Where? you might ask). Yes, I've been living here for the past 7 or 8 years of my life. But, I guess this is the closest place to ever feeling like home. Previously I have lived in Connecticut, Georgia,, and of course, Texas, but I had never been able to establish any lasting relationships.

Fortunately, from the time I was old enough to comprehend my parents explained to me about my adoption. Honestly I never wasreally bothered by this until a few years ago. I don't think I've ever had any resentment towards you, only questions. I want to know so many things about you, i.e.

1) What you look like?
2) What were you like growing up?

3) Do I have any siblings?- Perhaps brothers, I've always wanted a big brother. I feel I've missed out on a lot being an only child.
4) What are your dreams and fears?, etc.

I could go on forever, but I won't. After all, there are 15 years of built up questions waiting for someone to answer.

I totally realize that you probably have many other things to deal with, family, husband and probably painful memories. I want you to know even if you decide not to contact me , that I am so thankful to you for giving me life and choosing my parents. The last thing I want to do is to complicate or interfere in your life. I only hope and pray that the missing puzzle piece will want to be a part of my picture.

Sincerely, Jewel

Jewel and Erin spoke on the phone on 10/96 for the first time.

Dec. 1996
Dear Erin,

How are you? I'm doing pretty good , busy though. I first want to start out by saying how very sorry I am for taking so long to respond to your letter. I really hope you haven't taken it personally, but I've been just running around like a chicken with its head cut off lately. It's hard for me to believe Christmas will be here in about 2 weeks. (I have so much to do!) I really hope you had a nice thanksgiving, I did. We had about 30 people over at my house this year. Do you usually have large family gatherings for the holidays or is your family more widespread? Are there any special traditions your family has? I really enjoyed the pictures of Joey (author's note: Joey is Erin's son), he's a really cute kid. I would really enjoy some more pictures of you too. I've been meaning to tell you how much I did enjoy our conversation on the phone. It was really nice for me to place a voice with your face, which was a really important connection we made with each other, and I hope we can have another one in the near future.

So much has happened, it might take me a little while to fill you in on everything ...(Jewel tells Erin about what's been going on in her life)...

Well, I've got to get going, sorry again for not responding sooner. I feel really bad. I hope you have a Merry Christmas and a Happy New Year.

Love, Jewel

Jewel and Erin spoke again 4/97. They have not had direct contact yet. Jewel has told her parents she would like to correspond directly with Erin instead of going through an intermediary. Her parents are comfortable with this.

Letter from Adam, age 9, to his birthmother, Sherry, 7/91. (Sherry is the birthmom of both Adam and Aaron.)

Dear Sherry,

Do you have any pets? We have 5 dogs and 3 cats. I take karate. I am the best sparer in my division. I like to play sports. I've got a joke for you:

It's snowing. You go in a house there's a lamp, a stove and a fireplace. You have a match left. Which one should you light first? Answer on back.

Here are some things I'd like to know

> How tall are you?
> How old are you?
> What is your hobby?
> Are your neighbors nice?
> do you play sports?
> do you sew?

Love, Adam
(answer to the joke: the match)

Letter from Adam to Sherry 12/91

Dear Sherry
Hi how are you doing? I'm fine. On Nov. 27, 1991 8:AM we got on a plane to Dallas. Then we went to the Nursing Home where we saw Grandpa and the Grahams (note: these are birthrelatives) It would have been fun had you been there. After that we went to Six Flags.

Love Adam

Letter from Aaron, Adam's brother, age 11 to Sherry, his birthmother 7/91

Dear Sherry
How are you doing? I am fine. I miss you a lot. I am doing great in school. My friends at school and home are great! I am in karate. We have a lot of pets. I like to draw. I like chocolate. I like to make things with all kinds of stuff. I go to church every Sunday. We have a Nintendo & Game Boy. I have a brain buster for you. "If King Midas sits on gold who sits on Silver?" Hm. The Lone Ranger Ha! I love you.
   Do you live in an apartment or a house? How old are you? Are you tall or short? Is your hair long or short?

Love, Aaron

Letter from Aaron 12/91

Hi! I'm sorry I haven't written in such a long time, but I have been doing homework almost every day of the week. I have had a extra assignment almost every week.
   I am getting interested in girls. Do you have any tips or suggestions?
   I had a great time visiting our birthfamily, but it would have been better if you were there. I had a great time at Six Flags. We made a music video. We did "Can't touch this" by MC Hammer. He is my favorite rapper. What is your phone number? I really want to know.
   Have a Merry Christmas and a Happy New Year

Love Aaron

Letter from Lexie, age 5, to her birthmother, Michelle

Dear Michelle

Please write me

Love, Lexie   5

Excerpts of letters from Joy, age 14, to her birthmother, Caty

Dear Mom,
Before I start writing in length, I just wanted to say something I think
you should know. I want to say that this whole thing is probably just as
scary and confusing to me as it is to you. It took me 20 min. to decide
if I should put "Caty" or "Mom" after "Dear". You are like a giant
puzzle piece that's missing. My life will not be complete until I find
that piece.
    My name is Joy. I am 14 years old. I have medium length curly
dark brown hair. I have brown eyes, straight teeth, full lips and long
eyelashes. My face is very Spanish and African American looking.
People say I'm very pretty and I could be a great model. I'm 5'2 1/2"
(a shortie) and weigh 120. I have large muscles and broad shoulders. I
wear a size 8 and have a size 6 shoe.
    My hobbies are basically all having to do with music. My main
talent is singing. I've done many performances, solos duets and I'm in
one of the best choirs in ...I also swim and did gymnastics for 6 years
but quit in 1995. I also like to run. My life has been filled with hard
times and problems. I am clinically depressed and on anti depressant
for it. ...Many things have contributed to to my depression and anxiety.
when I was 8, my brother ...had cancer and died at age 10...Another
thing was not knowing my real mommy...But I am much better and in
counseling. ...Some people may think I have too much attitude but I
think being adopted has made me a very strong person. I make friends
easily and have had many boyfriends. I definitely want to go to college

and major in musical performance and minor in psychology...It has been very hard not knowing you. I don't mean to make you sad or angry. I just want to know who you are and where I really came from. I want to see my sister, aunts, uncles, cousins and grandparents. I also want to know more about my dad. I know you may not want to have any contact with me but my life will not be complete until I know you.

I love you,
Joy
PS I also was wondering what time I was born.
PPS I also have a sister...,2 brothers...

Letter from Joy to Caty and Caty's daughter, Jill 4/97

Dear Mom and Jill,
Before I start I want to say thank you for allowing me into your life. I was so scared that you might not want to communicate with me, but I knew inside that would be near impossible. I love you all, and I'm grateful. The pictures you sent were lovely. We have the same eyes and face shape. Everyone was shocked because you have red hair and I have dark brown! Jill is adorable! I have her picture along with yours hanging in my locker and bedroom. When I first got the pictures, I was filled with joy. I finally got to see a picture of the woman who created me.

The letter was incredible. I was filled with tears of joy when I read it. It's funny because we both have the same writing style. After my mother read it, she said, "so that's where you got your writing talent!" I guess so!

You answered so many of my questions. Now I understand what I need to do in order to overcome my problems...I want to make everyone proud of me-especially you...The part about your manic depression helped. ...

We have a big family! I don't have nearly as many cousins on both of my mom and dad's side combined.!!

......We have a smart family, also. You said many of my cousins went or are attending college- I am too!...Hope to hear from you soon With all my love, mom
Joy

Letter from Joy, July 1997

Dear Mom,
It was starting to seem as though we were losing touch so I am writing
to you and Jill. Before I begin I would like to inform you that I am a
very happy person!!!
　　I have been out of intensive treatment for depression...for over a
month now. I am much more happy now and am a healthy person,
more or less. I still have a couple of things to work on, but otherwise I
am great!! Everyone has commented on my happiness and that I
always have a smile on my face. I hope you are doing great and
remembering that I love you.
　　As for my singing and other activities, they are the best they have
ever been. I auditioned for a Youth Chorale at the ...Conservatory in
June...The conductor is a very, very serious and amazing musician...He
asked me if I could sing Gospel music. He said to sing Amazing grace
which is one of my favorites. I belted it out. I was amazed at what
came out of my mouth. He immediately said I was in...
　　How is Jill doing? Please tell her I said Hello and I love her.
...please let her know that I am not taking you away from her and that
we are both your daughters.. I do not want this process to harm your
relationship with Jill in any way. I don't have any other news to share
with you, so I will close. I hope to hear from you soon. Please give
everyone all my love.

Love always, Joy

Joy and Jill spoke on the telephone early Oct 97. Correspondence and
telephone contact will continue with the use of a professional
intermediary for now. This is what is comfortable for Joy's family.

Excerpts of first letter from boy to his birthmother. When the contact with his birthmother was initiated, Casey was still 17. He turned 18 shortly thereafter.

I must begin this letter with the biggest thanks possible. I have enjoyed an extraordinary and exciting life, a life that you began and a life that you shaped forever with your decision to pick the...agency to aid you in the search of proper parents. I strongly believe that the match was meant to be.

There are so many things I want to share with you. I am sure that this letter will only be the beginning, on that note we'll start from the beginning...(He shares events from his growing up years) .....

During my junior year however problems slowly began to crop up. I started to "branch out" into new and different things, little did I realize that I was only doing these things to be accepted by others—a fault that drove me to new heights. I decided one day to look down, to see what I had accomplished in my tree of the unknown. When I looked down I realized I had been falling, my journey had been taken for the wrong reasons. I discovered I was not looking for personal gratification, I never had been, I was simply doing things that were encouraged by others, I gave into peer pressure...My tree of the unknown had roots in the need to satisfy others...I decided to get away from most of my "friends"...I soon found myself going in the opposite direction, I was heading out of the pit and into the light...When I arrived on this side of everything I found a loving but weary mother. My entire family had scars, all received from their efforts to pull me up from the pit, hoping to get the rope to me before I hit bottom. So many times I saw that rope and so many times I cut that rope, denied that rope—in the end there were so many times that I hoped for that rope but I was left to my own devices to find a way out, and I did. Now I am busy exploring a new tree, rooted in my desire to do what is right for me, and what is right to do for others. It is in the light and it does require a little pruning but couldn't everyone's life use a little pruning?

You might be wondering how I came out after all of this. Well, in my estimation, just fine- better than that I think... So here I sit, a changed teenager who can say that he has been there and done that instead of saying that I go there and do that. I am presently experiencing the best time of my life...and my family life has never been better. I imagine that you might be asking why I wanted to contact you. Well, as I told you before I have begun to shape a new life for myself, and I now believe that I am emotionally and psychologically ready for this step in my life. I am a very curious person and for the past eighteen years I have lived not knowing what my parents looked like, where they came from, what they like, if I have any brothers or sisters etc. To give you an example of how little I have been told I recently learned that your first name is Jane, a fact that has (for some odd reason) amazed me. I am hungry for knowledge and for a friendship with the woman who gave birth to me. I do not expect to find a fairy god-mother who would bless me with a BMW, I really don't expect much of anything- but I do look forward to meeting you face to face for the second time.

I hope, and I am being completely sincere, that if this is not a good time for you to go through with this, please feel free to say so. I do not want, in any way, to force you into something that you are not ready to go through with. A friendship made on this basis would only hinder the overall process. If you feel you need to wait, wait. There is always tomorrow—today is never the end. As I mentioned above I do not expect anything...therefore I am only asking a simple question (I must admit, it is one of the most thought provoking "simple " questions that I have ever asked) the question goes like this Is now a good time to get in touch with you? ...

.....Thank you very much for reading this letter, Jane. I have enjoyed writing it and I hope that I have made a half-way decent impression of myself. Finally, I wanted to once again thank you- I believe you brought a pretty good guy into this world, and for that I will admire you forever....

Chapter 1

Opening Closed and Semi-Open Adoptions: A History

This book came into being to help people considering opening a closed or semi-open adoption. It will also be of assistance to families who have already accomplished this but who are seeking guidance about issues that arise as birthfamilies and adoptive families get acquainted.

In closed adoptions there is usually no contact between the birth and adoptive families. Today, information is sometimes passed on through a third party. The type of information considered safe and proper to pass on tends to be medical. Otherwise, it is frequently considered against the rules of a closed adoption to intrude on the lives of adoptive parents and birthparents by giving or asking for more information from either party.

Semi-open adoptions usually involve some sort of contact between adoptive and birthparents through a third party. This may include an exchange of letters, pictures and gifts. Some of the families in semi-open adoptions have even met one another one or more times. However, there usually is no sharing of last names, telephone numbers or addresses.

The practice of open adoption, which involves direct contact between adoptive families and birthfamilies, has been widespread for many years now. In open adoption the two families meet one another, share names and addresses and are able to be in touch with each other over the years. The people involved decide how often contact occurs.

Even though open adoptions have existed for many years, there is still a hesitation to change the way closed adoptions are handled. Feelings of concern about overstepping abound. Birthparents and adoptive parents are often afraid they may be asking for too much. At the same time, neither party wants to be pressed for more contact than is personally comfortable. Concerns about the effect on the adopted children are also typical.

This book will provide guidance to birth and adoptive families seeking to open their adoptions. Professionals involved in assisting them will also find the content helpful. The ultimate goal is to establish cooperative relationships between adoptive and birthfamilies. When this happens, everyone benefits, especially the children.

The opening of closed and semi open adoptions involves establishing a continuum, going from no direct contact to direct contact between birthfamilies and adoptive families of minor children (under 18 years). While most participants begin without knowledge of each other's identity, the typical cycle involves going from minimal to full awareness of each other's identity and location. The timing and specifics of this contact is determined by those involved.

The children whose adoptive parents have opted to open their adoptions range in age from infancy to adolescence. As the parents plunge into an adoption, they speak of wanting to anticipate their children's questions and needs before they are even expressed. These parents tend to be quite secure in their role of parenting through adoption. The fear of losing the children to the birthparents is less than in those parents who might not choose to explore direct contact.

When birthparents seek contact with their children, it is because they want to make themselves available, also anticipating the children's needs over time. They often express a profound need to know that the children are alive and well. Most respect the adoptive parents and don't wish to make them feel insecure. They try to be as non-threatening as possible, offering medical information, pictures, and letters.

It takes tremendous courage for birthparents to come forward. They, too, have heard the voices that have taught us about the realities of adoption. They have been told by agency professionals, friends, family, and society that they need to put the adoption behind them. They are frequently told: "It is done with, now move on." When they allow themselves to acknowledge that it is normal not to forget, they often make efforts to open their adoptions.

History of closed adoption

To put the trend toward open adoption into focus, it is useful to examine how we got here in the first place. Without this history, what we are doing might not seem necessary. The practice of adoption brought about the creation of new family units through the elimination of the original ones. The belief was that this was necessary for everyone's benefit, particularly adoptive family members, sparing them the risks of interference by the birthfamily.

When information about a birthfamily was gathered and shared with adoptive parents, it was usually done as briefly as possible. The thinking was that this would spare them the burden of knowing too much. Of course, no one imagined that adopted children would want to know anything. Medical concerns appeared to be insignificant as histories were barely gathered and certainly not updated. Somehow the unspoken assumption seemed to be that the medical history was also transferred to the adoptive parent realm. Once adopted, the child's medical history would be the same as the adoptive parents' histories. This sounds absurd, but this practice continues even today as families enter into closed adoptions receiving little or no information.

In the 1970s, adopted persons and birthparents began to speak out about how closed adoptions had affected them. Up until this time, it was believed that there were no problems with how adoptions were being handled. Adoptive families were considered to be pretty much like any other family. Adopted persons were supposed to be integrated into the adoptive family as though they had been born to the adoptive parents. Birthparents were expected to move on with their lives, leaving the adoption behind. Then, to everyone's amazement, those most affected clamored to be heard. Instead of a simple, problem-free journey, they described a complex and impacting life experience. Erosion of faithfully held beliefs began to occur, as triad members (birthparents, adoptive parents and adoptees) and professionals examined the practices which, for so many years, had promoted secrecy.

The adoption movement, at first made mostly up of adopted persons and birthparents, dramatically influenced the course of adoption practice. From the voices of adopted persons came the books *The Adopted Break Silence* by Jean Paton (1954) and *Twice Born: Memoirs of an Adopted Daughter* by Betty Jean Lifton (1975). One of the earliest books focusing on maintaining contact is *Open Adoption and Open Placement* (1981), co-authored by January Roberts and Diane Robie. Ms. Roberts is a birthmother who arranged an open adoption for her school age children and Ms. Robie is an adoptive mother who recognized her child's need to know his birthfamily. *The Adoption Triangle* by Sorosky, Baran, and Pannor (1979) and *Dear Birthmother* by Silber and Speedlin (1982), made a significant contribution from the professional arena.

Groups such as the American Adoption Congress and The Adoptee's Liberty Movement Association (ALMA) established large memberships. They responded to the needs of those touched by adoption

3

through newsletters, conferences and monthly meetings. Sometimes militant in their approaches, they left their mark and made society take note of what mattered when adoption is featured in one's life.

Cautiously, agencies arranging adoptions began to look at ways to increase the amount of information that was shared with birthparents and adoptive parents. They not only listened to triad groups and enlightened professionals, but also heard their own clients joining the voices for change. Gradually, open adoption began to evolve by establishing varying degrees of contact between adoptive families and birthfamilies. This is often described as openness in adoption.

The early stages of openness included letter writing through intermediaries, usually agency personnel. Some sharing of pictures and gifts occurred, at least at the early stages of the adoption. Today, this is often referred to as semi-open adoption. Sometimes these activities were only allowed for a brief time period as the mental health value of continued contact was questioned. This especially seemed to be centered on the concern that as the children got older that they would be confused by including birthparents in their lives.

The practice of open adoption went through dramatic shifts as the comfort level of those involved grew. Over a span of just a few years, the contacts went from being in touch without the sharing of identities, to face to face meetings. Eventually, people shared their identities with one another, exchanging names, addresses and phone numbers. This enabled them to establish contact without the involvement of agency personnel.

Open adoption as blended family

As noted in *Children of Open Adoption*, **"We began to recognize that open adoption was a new type of blended family."** We are all familiar with the concept of blended family. For example, families get rearranged through life events that lead to remarriage. It is well accepted that family restructuring makes life more complex. Moms move out, new brothers and sisters join in, extra grandparents appear, visits get worked out and so on.

While this is accepted in families brought together after divorce or death of a spouse, it is not typically accepted in families created by adoption. For some mysterious reason, the adoptive family is supposed to be the holdout for the perfect, imaginary family. The truth is, this does not exist. Yet, to allow imperfection in relationships joined by adoption is not tolerated by the community at large.

Many people express concern about problems that may arise when birthfamilies and adoptive families are in contact with one another. Pointing out that this is another form of family connection, and that all families deal with complexities, sometimes increases understanding. Nationally, through the 80's and 90's we have seen a steady increase in the number of blended-through-adoption families. These are created with the commitment to maintain contact with one another through the years. The nature and degree of this contact is being determined by those involved.

Families created through the closed adoption process have carefully followed the developments in open adoptions. Birthparents have observed how birthparents in open adoptions are updated regarding the growth and welfare of their children. While knowledge doesn't take away the grief or the loss of the separation, it does offer comfort and a greater peacefulness. The result has been that an increasing number of birthparents have come forward seeking to make themselves available to their children and their families.

Adoptive parents of minor children have also followed the developments in the changing practice. Additionally, as their children grew, they heard them express questions and needs related to their birthfamilies. The belief had been that going from one family to another was easy. Instead, they began to understand how complicated it is for the children, themselves, and the birthparents. Furthermore, most realized that they were not prepared for what they experienced.

Families with semi-open adoptions also asked for more contact. Thus, as a natural outgrowth of the open adoption practice, the opening of closed and semi-open adoptions evolved.

In this book, we will examine this experience focusing on minor children as distinguished from the searches involving adults. Among the topics to be covered will be:

- who may initiate the request,
- getting professional assistance,
- preparing for contact,
- making contact,
- the role of commitment,
- when all isn't equal among adopted siblings,
- reopening open adoptions, and
- opening adoptions with special needs children.

5

Learning more about open adoption

Literature
There are a number of great ways to educate yourself on the ins and outs of open adoption. Books, newsletters and magazines offer a wealth of information on open adoption issues. Here are some of the best sources.

Books
A Letter to Adoptive Parents on Open Adoption by Randolph Severson. House of Tomorrow Productions, Dallas, TX, 1991. Avaliable through Heart Word Center, Dallas, TX. This 28 page booklet is a perfect introduction to adoptive parents on openness in adoption.

Children of Open Adoption by Kathleen Silber and Patricia Martinez Dorner. Corona Publishing, 1990. Finally, a book that answers questions about the effect of open adoption on the children. Two pioneers in the field examine scores of open adoption experiences from infancy to adolescence, including bonding, communication, entitlement, a child's understanding of adoption, and more. Easy to read.

Dear Birthmother by Kathleen Silber and Phylis Speedlin. Corona Publishing, 1983. A classic, this book examines the myths in adoption and lays the foundation for open adoption. Contains practical suggestions and guidance as well as letters between adoptive parents and birthparents.

The Open Adoption Experience by Lois Melina and Sharon Kaplan-Roszia. HarperPerennial, 1993. A complete guide for both birthfamilies and adoptive families. Covers topics from readiness for open adoption to growing up in an open adoption. Co-written by two leaders in the field of adoption, this book is not only must-reading for those considering open adoption, but also a handy reference book as the child grows.

The Spirit of Open Adoption by James Gritter. Child Welfare League of America, 1997. This book goes beyond the basics to explore the philosophy and deeper meaning that all triad members can experience by participating in an open adoption. A ground-breaking book.

6

Magazines and newsletters

Adopted Child. Published monthly and edited by Lois Melina, this four page newsletter offers professionally written and researched information on issues effecting the adopted child. Adopted Child Publications, P.O. Box 9362, Moscow, ID, 83843. Telephone: (208) 882-1794. e-mail: lmelina@moscow.com

Adoptive Families. A full color magazine that covers all aspects of adoption. Articles written primarily to an adoptive parent audience, but has some articles of interest to birthparents. Adoptive Families, 3333 Hwy. 100 North, Minneapolis, MN 55422. Telephone: (612) 535-4829.

Adoption with Heart and Soul. Edited by Randolph Severson and published twice a year. Discusses reform and ethics in adoption in an accessible style. Address: 4054 McKinney Ave, Suite 302, Dallas, TX 75204. Telephone: (214) 5214560.

Open Adoption Birthparent. Quarterly newsletter edited by Brenda Romanchik, a birthmother in an open adoption. Covers all aspects of birthparenthood in an open adoption situation. Open to adoption professionals and all triad members. R-Squared Press, 721 Hawthorne, Royal Oak, MI 48067. Telephone: (810) 543-0997. email: brenr@oeonline.com

PACT Press. Quarterly newsletter that covers all aspects of inter-racial adoption including open adoptions. Has articles of interest for all triad members. PACT Press, 3315 Sacramento, San Fransisco, CA 94118. Telephone: (415) 221-6957.

Roots and Wings. Quarterly magazine that focus on all aspects of adoption. Written primarily for an adoptive parent audience. Roots and Wings, P.O. Box 638, Chester, NJ 07930. Telephone: (908) 637-8899.

Open adoption agencies

When looking for an agency, be sure to specify that you are interested in hearing about open adoption families that will have contact with one another. Many agencies promote open adoption but use a more limited definition that includes anything from meeting and exchanging non-identifying information before the birth, to the exchange of pictures and letters through the agency after the birth. You can also contact Jim Gritter of the American Association of Open Adoption Agencies at Catholic Human Services, 1000 Hastings, Traverse City, MI 49684, telephone (616) 947-8110, to find an agency in your area. The National Federation for Open Adoption Education, may also know of an agency in your area. Call them at (510) 827-2229.

Conferences

Adoption conferences are also a good way to further educate yourself on open adoption issues. Not only do they allow you to hear what the experts have to say, but they also provide the opportunity for you to meet other adoptive parents and birthparents living the open adoption experience. There are a number of national conferences as well as regional conferences that address open adoption issues. Adoptive Families Magazine has a fairly complete listing of current conferences. The following are four national conferences that focus solely on open adoption.

Biennial Conference on Open Adoption. This conference has on its faculty the best minds in open adoption thought and practice. Sponsored by Catholic Human Services in Traverse City, this conference is geared toward professionals, birthparents and adoptive parents in open adoptions. It has a general session format. Although it is a bit off the beaten path, it is a conference well worth attending. It is held in mid-spring every other year. For more information, contact Jim Gritter, Child Welfare Supervisor, Catholic Human Services, 1000 Hastings, Traverse City, MI 49684. Telephone: (616) 947-8110.

Biennial Conference on Open Adoption Families. Held on the off year of the Biennial Conference on Open Adoption, this conference focuses on the ongoing issues that all those involved open adoption face. A wonderful gathering for professionals, birthparents, adoptive parents and the children they love. For more information, contact Brenda Romanchik, R-Squared Press, 721 Hawthorne, Royal Oak, MI 48067. Telephone: (248)543-0997.

Lifegiver's Festival. This annual conference is exclusively for birthparents in open adoptions. It's informal structure allows birthparents to focus on the issues most important to them. It is sponsored by Catholic Human Services of Traverse City, MI and R-Squared Press. It is held in

October. For more information, contact Brenda Romanchik, R-Squared Press, 721 Hawthorne, Royal Oak, MI 48067. Telephone: (248)543-0997.

National Open Adoption Conference. Sponsored by The National Federation for Open Adoption Education, this conference is geared primarily toward professionals, but triad members are encouraged to attend. It is generally held in early November of each year. For more information contact the federation at: 391 Taylor Blvd., Suite 100, Pleasant Hill, CA 94523. Telephone: (510) 827-2229.

Adoption education and support groups

Adoption education and support groups are an invaluable community resource. Not only do they provide an opportunity to get to know others in your area, but they also provide information on other local adoption resources and referrals to therapists that specialize in adoption. Most are listed in the yellow pages under adoption, but you can also get a complete listing for your state by contacting the National Adoption Information Clearinghouse (see page 22 for details.)

Chapter 2

Why Open an Adoption?

Closed adoption, by definition, does not provide a pathway for contact between adoptive families and birthfamilies. The central beliefs underlying this practice have now been redefined as myths by those involved in adoption. In the book, *Dear Birthmother*, Silber and Speedlin identify four core myths that drove the practice of adoption:

1. The birthmother obviously doesn't care about her child or she wouldn't have given her away. Birthparents have taught us that they love their children, experiencing tremendous grief and loss for which they were not prepared. They didn't give away their children. Instead, they followed the path that society carved out for them. Most were unmarried parents and raising a child this way was not accepted in years past. Even today, when single parenting is everywhere, lack of readiness to parent is a frequent reason to choose adoption. Expressions of love, caring, and concern are ever present. While separating from one's kin translates to a lack of caring in our society, what we have learned about birthparents denies this.

2. There is only one proper way to place a child for adoption— veiled in secrecy. Mental health professionals tell us that secrets are not healthy. They create a huge number of problems for those involved. How then, do we justify a whole method of practice based on secrecy, no matter what the reason? "The truth shall set you free" is a popular expression that calls for truth - except when it involves adoption. Why would it not be healthy for this people who are involved in adoption too?

The secrecy which is such a big part of closed adoptions frequently creates a rift between birthparents and adoptive parents. Birthparents often have fears about what adoptive parents may be saying to their children about them. Adoptive parents fear the birthparents may want to take the children back. Reassuring each other of their good intentions is not possible. In most states adoption records are sealed by law. This usually includes the court and original birth certificate records. This, of course, further blocks birth and adoptive parents from making contact with one another, since they don't know each other's identity.

Closed adoption records were originally intended to protect the child from others finding out the facts of his birth. In a time when out-of-wedlock births were not tolerated, secrecy became the norm. This later became a way to "protect" the adoptive parent from birthparent kidnappings and interference. For some reason, it was believed that, while birthparents were forgetting their children, they were also busy planning their kidnapping!

We have come to learn that secrecy blocks access to one's truth. The need to know about one another became the clear message from the hearts and souls of those who pleaded for change. We have learned that healing and wholeness become possible when secrecy is replaced with access to one another.

3. Both the birthmother and birthfather will forget about their unwanted child. The belief that birthparents forget their children became another indication of their lack of caring since, after all, these children were unloved and unwanted. This myth appears to be a protective message for adoptive parents to enable them to feel more secure in their role. The chance of birthparents wanting to reclaim their children diminishes when these children are believed to be unwanted and forgotten. The message also discounts birthparent emotions and deals with them as only temporarily significant. Since birthparents are seen as necessary only until they provide a child to those more worthy adoptive parents, the hidden message is, "thank you for your baby, now get lost."

Each birthparent develops her own way of coping with her loss. Forgetting is not one method. It is impossible to wipe out nine months of carrying a child within. It was typical to give the mother drugs during delivery to try to block out the reality of the child. Preventing her from seeing her child after birth was part of this effort. These methods were touted as desirable for the birthmother so that separating from her child would be easier and she would not get attached to the born baby. The hidden agenda often was to disconnect her when she was most vulnerable—after delivery—to make sure the adoption happened.

Now for the truth. Birthparents never forget their children but hope that their lives are flourishing in their adoptive homes. The first words out of a birthmother often are: "How is he? They told me I would forget, but I never did."

The effects of birthparenthood include extreme feelings of grief, guilt, diminished self concepts, difficulty in trusting relationships due to their loss, and more. The closed adoption system cuts off contact with a significant person and allows no avenue for knowing about his welfare. While semi-open adoptions offer some levels of contact, there are shortcomings because the two families can't communicate with each other directly. It is important to point out that open adoption does not eliminate the emotions described above. However, they become more manageable when all the people involved have pathways for open communication.

It surprises adopted persons, who expect to be forgotten, that their birthdays, Mother's and Father's Day, and other family-centered holidays are tremendously difficult for birthparents. While birthparents remember their children throughout the year, these are dates that are particularly emotional. In my experience, about 90% of birthparents are open to contact, a fact that stuns those who believe the uncaring and forgetting myths.

4. If the adoptee loved his parents, he would not have to search for his birthparents. Adoptive families were supposed to be perfect families with no adoption-related needs. Therefore an adopted person who searches could not possibly love her adoptive parents. Something had to be wrong with the love bonds. In fact, most adopted persons will say, "I love my adoptive parents and my search is a search for myself." The need to connect with one's origins is totally normal. Being cut off from one's family is what is not normal. In the mental health world, cutting one's family off is seen as unhealthy. When examining family histories, counselors look at what family members have been cut off or blackballed. This becomes a point of focus in the counseling. Why, then, do we continue to treat adopted people differently as though, for them, this is healthy?

Many adopted persons have lost the courage to search by being put on the defensive when questioned about the ties to their adoptive parents. They are blocked from achieving the wholeness that is found when reconnecting with birthparents. They express a fear of hurting their parents. Often below the surface is a deeper fear, the fear of losing their adoptive parents. They know how deeply it hurts to have lost their first parents. Interwoven in this is also the fear of being rejected by the birthparents. Those who don't search often deny a need to search.

Instead, they focus on not wanting to hurt their adoptive parents or intrude on their birthparents.

This last myth is also a burden for adoptive parents. If the need to search relates to being unloved by their children, then, for many, their reason for being is threatened. They question their parenting, thereby feeding self doubt. These may be the parents who say to their children "How can you do this to me?" To them it is a public avowal of not being loved and therefore a failure at parenting. The insecurities of adoptive parenting often reach a peak during a search. They expect to be abandoned by their children. The fear that has always walked with them about losing their children to the birthparents is finally about to come true. Or so they think.

Instead, what we have learned is that through the search the adopted person is strengthened and his relationship with his adoptive parents gets even better than it was before. A whole person has more of himself to offer to others. When parents trust the love bonds that they have with their children, they are better able to give encouragement for a search. This is one of the most significant gifts they can give their children.

As more was learned about adoption and changes in practice happened, families entering adoptions began to have choices as openness evolved. That, individuals locked into closed adoptions would reevaluate their paths, is hardly surprising. Many of them came to realize that they wanted to eliminate the secrecy and fear from their adoptions. It became clear that the way to do this was through direct contact with one another. Redefining the essence of adoption as non-adversarial has led to a safer perception of the potential risks. The need to know the truth, to lay eyes on significant others and to get answers, will provide many the dignity to risk moving into opened adoptions.

The benefits of opening an adoption

Opening an adoption allows the child, as well as his birth and adoptive families, to address adoption issues as they come up. Problems, concerns and questions can be dealt with in an open, honest manner. Correct and updated information can be exchanged as needed. This can include medical information, on-going information about the two families, topics focusing on adoption matters and more. All of this helps families to be supportive to each other and to get to know each other in a meaningful and personal way. They no longer have to wonder about or fear each other.

Benefits for the adopted child

When birthparents and adoptive parents know each other and no longer see each other as a threat, they are more likely to honor the place that each has in the child's life. Instead of competing with each other for the child's affection, they can now allow the child to love them all. This frees the child and diminishes loyalty conflicts. It doesn't mean they totally disappear, but they can be addressed directly when they happen. Witnessing the ties between the two sets of parents permits the child to give and accept love from all of them.

Feelings of rejection and abandonment are consistently expressed by adopted persons. Children begin to deal with these adoption issues at very young ages. (See *Talking to Your Child About Adoption*, for ages and stages). Preschoolers and school age children wonder what was wrong with them that their birthparents did not want them. From the adult perspective we know that that is incorrect thinking. However, a child that can't get the reassurance from his birthparent that he was not at fault, feels pain, and tends to blame himself. This tends to build layers of hurt that grow as the years pass. The hurt continues to deepen. The earlier the reconnection, hopefully, fewer layers are able to form. Having birthparents who are able to show their love and commitment by being in touch, allows the children to begin to heal. Again, this does not mean that these issues disappear, but that they become more manageable over time.

The break in the relationship between children and their birthparents created by closed and semi-open adoptions can severely affect the child's ability to trust. This has to do with the massive loss that adoption represents in the child's life. The effect of loss on the ability to trust is well documented in the literature and research about loss and grief. This is supported by adopted persons who regularly admit that trusting others is difficult.

When trust is lacking, it is difficult to connect to others because there is an ongoing fear that those we love will leave us. Therefore, bringing the birthparents back into the child's life can increase his ability to trust and develop significant love bonds with others. By not waiting until adulthood for the reconnection to happen, a multitude of relationships have a chance to be better cemented for the child. Attachment depends on the glue that connects at the heart. The continued involvement of birthparents and other birthfamily creates increased trust in the permanence of all relationships.

As mentioned above, loss of birthfamily deeply affects the adopted child. As one would expect, this loss creates feelings of grief. With the help of both set of parents, the child is able to address these issues, as needed, over time. Having access to birthparents often enables the adopted child to express his feelings more freely. This is because the message to the child is that adoption does play a significant part in his life and that the parents will help him walk through whatever arises.

These children have parents who are usually able to handle the visible and undercurrent grief, allowing the children to express it without feeling guilty. While it can be very painful to witness a child in grief, sharing these moments of intense emotion will help the child feel understood and supported. In the process, the parents build empathy for what the children are feeling. I have found that these shared moments increase the bonds of emotional attachment between children and their parents. Both birthparents and adoptive parents need to be open to the questions and emotions that occur as children work through these issues.

Sometimes adoptive parents have said that they had discouraged adoption talk because it made them feel badly that they had so little information to give their children. Likewise, the children have commented that they seldom discussed adoption since their questions seldom had answers. I have found that conversations about adoption tend to increase when information is more readily available.

Just the fact that adoptive parents and birthparents are linked for the child's good is an indication to the child that adoption is an O.K. subject. When questions arise for which the adoptive parents have no answer, it is a simple matter to ask birthparents or other birthfamily members. The child is able to concretely witness the comfort levels of both sets of parents as they deal with each other.

As the child gets a sense of self derived from both his family trees, his self concept gets stronger. He no longer has to waste energy wondering about where he came from, why he was adopted, whether his birthparents love and remember him, etc. Instead, he can obtain answers as needed. It is interesting to note that, as the contact becomes more established, that the children become very matter-of-fact about it. It becomes normal and natural, similar to what happens in families that have always been in touch.

Benefits to birthparents

There is so much that birthparents do not know about their children when they are in closed and semi-open adoptions. This gnaws at their well being, leaving them with a sense of dis-ease. Birthparents benefit by knowing that their children are alive and well. The burdens that are lifted by the ongoing awareness of how the child is doing was described by a birthmother when she learned some news of her 16 year old son, "I feel as though I have received rubies! For the first time, I didn't go into deep depression on his birthday."

Birthparents also process grief and loss issues up close. Witnessing the child in the flesh puts into clearer focus the lost opportunity to parent the child and the missed moments (first words, steps, beginning school etc.). Sometimes they report having feelings of regret about the adoption, even though they realize that, at the time of the decision, they may not have had another option. They will also speak of feeling jealous of the adoptive parents and the part they have in the children's lives. The benefit of having direct contact is that birthparents are able to move through these feelings to a greater acceptance that adoption is a reality in their lives.

Part of the healing journey requires getting in touch with the grief, which is often very intense as the child becomes increasingly real in the mind of the birthparent. Being acknowledged as important in the child's life, even if not in a parenting role, has a healing quality.

Just as adopted persons need to know why the adoption took place, the birthparents have an equal need to tell them the "whys." As they are able to accomplish this, the guilt they usually feel, begins to be reduced. This happens because the child is usually not judgmental even when he feels his own pain related to the adoption. Being able to watch the emotions that are shown by birthparents helps shift feelings of abandonment and rejection to a sense of truly being loved. This mutual process of healing happens gradually and has far reaching impact. The results are strengthening for both parties.

Benefits to adoptive parents

Adoptive parents benefit in that they feel more entitled to parent their children. The birthparents can directly give them their blessing to do the best job they know how. When they can communicate directly, they can see that they don't have to spend their lives being scared of birthparents. The message they receive, both through words and actions, is that they have nothing to fear. There is no kidnapping plan. There is only the hope on the part of birthparents to remain included in the extended family picture.

Sometimes adoptive parents worry that, by including birthparents in their lives, they are leaving themselves open to co-parenting. They often have concerns about being judged about the way they are raising their children. What they discover is that birthparents are usually very respectful of the adoptive parents' place as the parents. This is very reassuring to adoptive parents; it helps them feel like they have the right to be the parents who make the parenting decisions.

Most adoptive parents have had problems with infertility. We now understand that coming to terms with the grief that results is vital in dealing with adoption. It is normal for prospective parents to imagine the characteristics of a child they hope will be born to them. When they are not able to bear children, part of the grieving involves putting this fantasy child to rest. This doesn't mean that the hurt and disappointment will disappear. However, unless these feelings are in a more peaceful place, the child they adopt runs the risk of being compared with the imaginary, nonexistent child. This makes it difficult to accept the adopted child and all his unique attributes.

By including birthparents in their lives, they directly face that their child was born to someone else. This allows for infertility issues to be addressed honestly rather than buried in denial. There is an opportunity for a more peaceful coexistence with this truth.

As adoptive parents get to know the birthfamilies of their children, they begin to recognize how genes play a big part in who we are. Sometimes adoptive parents and their children are so different from one another, that understanding one another can be difficult.

The more the birthfamily is understood, the more this assists in parenting efforts. Patterns of behavior, tastes, and special talents in their children that may have seemed unusual, make more sense to adoptive parents once they see these traits in the birthfamily. The wonderful benefit is that adoptive parents gain a better understanding of their children and can, therefor, do a better job of parenting them.

Another area that is affected by contact has to do with fantasies adoptive parents have about birthparents. Contact allows them to deal with the realities. Adoptive parents who previously believed that birthparents don't care or are busy forgetting their children, are no longer able to hold on to the fantasy because they are able to see how much they care. These safeguards to parenthood are no longer needed because they feel safer. Instead, a relationship can develop on whatever terms are possible that allows for everyone to have a place. When a friendship can develop between the adults, everyone benefits.

It is important to point out that the relationships being described here do not have to be perfect because there is no such thing. Additionally, the profound and complex adoption issues won't disappear for any of the parties. However, by identifying birth and adoptive families as family, substantial benefits can be derived by all involved. The goal is to do everything possible to create a healthy environment for the growing child and the adults who surround him.

Initiating requests

Seventeen years of deep immersion in opening closed adoptions have convinced me that requests can appropriately originate with either the birthfamily or the adoptive parents. Usually the birthfamily focus is on the birthmother exclusively. However, there are an increasing number of birthfathers who are coming forward making themselves available both initiating the request and accepting the approach. As in all relationships, boundaries must be respected by the participants. What this means, is that whatever evolves, happens through mutual agreement, holding the best interest of the child as central.

It is vital to pay attention to the manner in which the desired contact is presented. The old rules about closed adoption tend to lurk, frequently striking fear especially in the hearts of adoptive parents. It is useful to frame the outreach as an invitation to participate and an opportunity to learn more about one another. Reassuring those approached that privacy can be maintained, is also important. We must remember that even though a child is shared by the birth and adoptive parents that they don't know each other. Therefore they will need to learn how to communicate with one another.

I have found that when courteous and respectful rules of friendship are observed, the results tend to be positive. Often the two families will have very different life experiences and ways of dealing with the world. Being aware of this is helpful in building an understanding of one another. An exchange in one family may have a very different significance in the other. Learning to understand one another correctly is an important part of developing a good relationship.

The concept of the blended family acknowledges not only the adoptive parents and birthparents, but also other extended family members. In some cases, extended birthfamily members become more actively involved than the birthparents. Even though adopted children tend to focus their needs primarily on birthparents and siblings, evaluating relatives who wish to commit to contact over time is important. This is especially true when the birthparents are unwilling or unable to come forth. Mutual appreciation of both family trees contributes to including as many relatives as wish to participate. As in all relationships, chemistry and affinity will play a part in the developing bonds once contact occurs.

When is it not indicated to open an adoption?

There may be times when establishing contact may not be indicated. If there is any concern about the safety of those involved, one may choose to maintain a level of contact where identities and locations are not shared. Even when there is a criminal history or mental illness, I have seen contact succeed when some safeguards are built in. For example, there may be letter writing, but no meetings in person. This may continue until a level of trust is reached which would allow for more contact. By setting workable limits, the relationship may have a chance to grow. In these cases, it may be wise to use an experienced professional who can evaluate the situation. In most instances, at least some level of contact can successfully occur.

Sometimes adoptive parents seeking contact have a hidden agenda when their child is having serious problems. They may hope that the birthparent may take over the raising of the child. These often were the parents who feared that the birthparents would kidnap their children and now they wish they would! Caution is important here and opening the adoption on this basis is probably a poor idea. There are situations where the birthparents have helped out temporarily, but this is not the usual way it happens. Birthparents wish to be resources for their children, but they are not typically seeking to parent or reclaim custody.

Another situation where caution is advised is if a birthparent seems focused on reclaiming the child. We are not talking about a birthparent reconsidering the adoption decision during the time allowed by law. It is very different when a birthparent of an infant reconsiders the original decision as provided by the law, as opposed to a birthparent of a school aged child, where disruption of the adoption would have serious ramifications. There *are* birthparents who feel deep regret about their decision, but this does not mean that they want to reclaim their children. Sometimes adoptive parents have a hard time understanding a birthparent's regret and link it with a belief that the birthparent wants the child back. Fortunately, in most situations, these scenarios are not typical. Most parties wish to interweave their lives rather than eliminate the other parents, whether they be adoptive or birthparents. There may be situations when establishing contact is indicated but only with the support of therapy. Examples of this would be a child actively abusing drugs or alcohol, or a child with serious emotional problems. When a troubled child is in counseling, it is possible to deal with whatever troubles him about his adoption. The child who is acting out is often struggling with adoption issues but he may not be admitting it. Therefore, opening an adoption at this time gives him the chance to deal with his adoption in a safe and supported way. Frequently it is assumed that a troubled child can't handle the link with birthfamily because it would just make matters worse.

The truth is that adoption is always a core issue for children and that it plays a role when children are struggling with life. Too often, during therapy, adoption becomes overlooked or its importance minimized. This is a serious oversight. It is recommended that therapists who have experience with adoption be used so as to increase the benefits of therapy. At the same time, it is important to note that opening the adoption is not a magical cure-all. What it does offer is the opportunity to address important developmental issues over time and turn some corners. It also makes it possible to bring one's needs out into the open in a safe and supported way.

It is an oversimplification to assume that contact necessarily changes the path of problematic children. In summery, there will be times when adoptions should not be opened or should have some safeguards included. As we said before, even when there are problems the opening of an adoption may offer a turning point in the lives of those involved.

Resource: The National Adoption Information Clearinghouse (NAIC)

The National Adoption Information Clearinghouse (NAIC) was established by Congress to provide professionals and the general public with easily accessible information on all aspects of adoption, including open adoption. NAIC maintains an adoption literature database, a database of adoption experts, listings of adoption agencies, crisis pregnancy centers, and other adoption-related services, and excerpts of state and federal laws on adoption.

The NAIC is a valuable resource for those seeking to open an adoption. They provide free information on a wide variety of topics including:

- search information,
- open adoption,
- the impact of adoption on birthparents,
- state-by-state adoption laws
- adoption and stages of development, and
- answers to children's questions about adoption.

They also have a number of publications and catalogs that you can purchase, including a catalog of audio-visual materials on adoption ($15), and provide referrals to therapists that specialize in adoption issues as well as referrals to search and support groups.

Contact them at PO Box 1182, Washington, DC 20013-1182, telephone 703-352-3488 or 888-251-0075, fax 703-385-3206, e-mail naic@calib.com, or on the World Wide Web at http://www.calib.com/naic.

Adoption on the Internet

The Internet has a wealth of information available, quite literally, at your finger tips. If you do not have your own Internet account, many libraries now have web access. Without your own e-mail address, however, you will not be able to subscribe to the mailing lists.

A word of caution. While many sites, mailing lists and Usenet groups may seem like an intimate setting, there are hundreds, if not thousands of people that have access to them. Please do NOT use the full names and addresses of others without their permission. There have been a couple of cases where identifying information was shared with disastrous results.

Web sites

http://www.plumsite.com/adoptionring/ring.shtml
The Adoption Ring is a public service ring dedicated to the best interests of adoption triad members. It is an ever expanding group of over 100 pages designed to allow web surfers to navigate to pages of other not-for-profit adoption sites. Sites of interest include search, support and activism sites for all triad members.

http://www.openadoption.org/
This is the site for the American Association for Open Adoption Agencies, and organization that is working towards developing high standards for open adoption practice. Highlights include: What Open Adoption is Not, The Support for Open Adoption Found In Current Research, and A Statement of Beliefs - A formula for adoption quality.

http://www.plumsite.com/isrr/
The International Soundex Reunion Registry is the world's largest reunion registry and is a free service. This registry does not perform a search or provide search advice. What it does provide is a place for birthparents, adult adoptees and the adoptive parents of minors to register in order to find one another.

http://www.geocities.com/CapitolHill/9606/mainsearchpage.html
This page has lots of information for those searching including links to: Adoption Forums, Registries and Reunion information, Online Data Bases, Social Security Information, State Information (including open

legislation information) and Statistics on Adoption.

Mailing lists

Birthmothers
A mailing list for birth mothers only is up and running and ready to help birth mothers who are looking for support and friendship. Head to http://www.eden.com/~belinda/ for information on subscribing to the list and for birth mother resources.

Birthmothers in semi-open and open adoptions
A mailing list for birthmothers in both open and semi-open adoptions. This list also has been known to welcome birthfathers and extended birthfamily by request. To subscribe send your request to:

OpenBmoms@Majordomo.net

Leave the subject field blank and in the body of the message type your command "subscribe". If you wish to receive the mailing list in digest format, type your command "subscribe digest".

Open adoption
There is a list for all triad members which focuses upon open adoptions. Write to Yvette Carter (ycarter@world.std.com) or Teri Liston (MeriOne@eworld.com) for more information. A very good list.

Adoption
The Adoption Triad mailing list is open to all members of the triad. Discussions involve a wide variety of adoption issues. To subscribe, send email to listserv@maelstrom.stjohns.edu with the following as the only text in your message: subscribe adoption FirstName LastName. Also a very good list.

Usenet newsgroups
Another Internet search resource would be the Usenet Newsgroups. Here are a couple of adoption-related groups available to all members of the triad. (Note, some browsers do not allow you to read newsgroups.)

alt.adoption.
This is a general discussion group open to all members of the triad, and the general public.

alt.adoption.agency.
Prospective and current adoptive parents may find assistance in the Usenet Newsgroup

Also check out the National Adoption Information Clearinghouse's new publication: Adoption Guide To The Internet. The 100-plus page Guide, available in a printed bound version or on 3.5 inch PC-compatible disk, lists over 500 Internet addresses, sponsors, and site description. The listings are arranged by category, enabling users to easily find material in a specific area of interest. Sections include: federal government agencies, federally funded clearinghouses and resource centers, state-specific information sites, licensed private agencies, search resources, support groups, electronic mailing lists, news groups, and bulletin boards. The guide is available for $10, which includes postage and handling, from NAIC, P.O. Box 1182,Washington DC, 20013-1182. Orders must be paid by check or money order before shipment.

Chapter 3

Getting Professional Assistance

It has been interesting to note the development of post-adoption services being provided by professionals. Among those frequently offered are support groups, registries, search assistance and information contained in adoption files. The extent of information shared from files is usually defined by agency philosophy and internal policy. Sometimes state law governs what is provided. For example, in Texas, agency files must be furnished, with identifying information removed, to adoptive parents and adopted adults.

Information given to birthparents regarding the adoptive family is often more limited in scope. In Texas and many other states, no law directly addresses what may be shared with birthparents about the adoptive parents of their children or about the children themselves. (There have been some changes in the Texas state guidelines that direct agencies to notify birthparents when their children die.) The result is that there is a tremendous amount of variation as to what birthparents may or may not receive. At the very least, they should receive the papers that they signed and ones they filled out. It is certainly advisable for birthparents to ask for as much as possible including updated information about their children and pictures that may be contained in the files.

There are situations whereby birthparents can't even find out the sex of their children. This is especially so in private adoptions. The reasons that are given often focus on privacy issues defined by the custodians of records. They cite confidentiality promised to all parties.

As long as closed records exist, those who have arranged the original adoption usually feel bound by the law to withhold identities. What seems to be overlooked is that confidentiality is not breached when an intermediary makes the contact without disclosing identities to those searching. This gives the intermediary the chance to find out if contact is desired by both parties. When this is the case, information and/or identities can be revealed. If contact is not wished at that time, confidentiality is preserved.

Since current adoption practice involves greater levels of openness, it is not out of line for agencies and lawyers to consider offering choices to past clients. Rather than assuming that everyone involved does not want contact, an outreach effort is possible to check this out. This allows the adoptive and birthparents to make decisions on their own behalf rather than allowing third parties this privilege.

There are adoption professionals, typically agency related, who will do searching on behalf of the adopted person but not on behalf of the birthparent. It would be wise to examine what message is projected as one portion of the triad is served and not the other. How do mental health workers make determinations about relative importance when there are three parties to be considered? After all, the model that guides the mental health field involves listening to clients' expressed needs. Why wouldn't an effort at least be made to create a bridge between adoptive and birthfamilies when they can't do it themselves because of closed records?

In light of this, the reality is that many facilitators of the original adoption are not willing to open closed adoptions. Options then, must be pursued. One avenue is to seek court access to the identifying information. There are an increasing number of judicial jurisdictions where the judges are well educated about adoption issues and will open the records. Here, too, there is a greater inclination to open the records to adoptive parents and not to birthparents.

Search groups are also often used to locate the necessary information. There are many, however, that will not get involved with minor searches, especially those initiated by birthparents. The concern here is that there is a risk that the birthparent will approach the child first and bypass the adoptive parents. If that were the case, the position of search groups would be wise because minor children are appropriately in the care of their parents and this relationship should not be violated. Inclusion of adoptive parents for a contact is vital. In my experience, birthparents are very respectful of adoptive parents and usually do not consider contacting the child first.

When people resort to judicial action or search groups, they are often already frustrated by the lack of responsiveness on the part of the agency or lawyer that arranged the adoption. Doctors and attorneys who originally acted as facilitators in arranging adoptions are not usually assisting in the reconnection process. Frequently they are still functioning by the belief system of the past invoking and maintaining secrecy. On the positive side, there has been a dramatic increase in the number of agencies assisting in these ventures.

Once records are obtained, one may choose to seek out the sought party oneself, use a professional intermediary or a self help search group. It is important to emphasize again that opening adoptions involves many complex issues. The more one prepares and learns about these, the higher the chances that it will go well. Those of you reading this book are already doing that. It would also be a good idea to talk to others who have already opened their adoptions. Support groups are also valuable so that there can be an exchange of ideas and experiences.

How to choose a professional

Due to the many issues involved, it is wise to consider professional involvement. Choosing someone who is familiar with the shadings and stages of the opening process would be advisable. Experienced professionals can recognize usual and unusual happenings. They can also help you look at surface and deeper issues. It allows for a wiser and safer journey.

How does one find such a professional? Usually they are not found in the ranks of general therapists. The specialty of adoption is still a developing one for clinicians outside of adoption agencies. Experienced providers can be found by networking organizations such as The Michigan Association for Openness in Adoption, The National Federation for Open Adoption Education and The National Adoption Information Clearinghouse.

Many agencies providing post-adoption services only serve their own clients. The benefits of this is that sometimes birthparents and adoptive parents have stayed in touch with agency personnel so that an on-going relationship is already established. This can be helpful during the course of opening an adoption, as people tend to feel more understood and supported. Having some knowledge of the agency professional will help families assess if they want to use that person or not. When an intermediary is used, a great deal depends on his ability to handle situations that come up.

Sometimes going back to the original agency is emotionally loaded, especially for birthparents. They associate the agency with the loss of their children and it is just too painful to deal with that agency again. When that is the case, it may be wise to seek services elsewhere.

At the same time, it is important to bear in mind that now the focus is different. Where before an adoption separation was about to happen, this time the goal is to establish contact. Because of this, it could be that using the original agency could work out in a positive way. The most important thing is to feel trust in whomever is going to act as an intermediary if one is going to be used.

The role of professionals

Many families decide to involve professionals in opening their adoptions because they feel they need the help of an experienced person. Obviously, one would want to use someone who can recognize what is normal or unusual in such a contact. The professional chosen would be someone who really understands adoption issues and believes that direct contact is desirable.

The professional as an intermediary

The professional is the intermediary when he is the voice between the two families opening an adoption. He usually locates and contacts the family being approached. As long as there is no direct contact, he is helping the two families find ways to communicate that are mutually comfortable. He is also helping them decide when they are ready to be in touch without his involvement. The professional intermediary needs to have skills in searching and in establishing and facilitating contact.

The professional as facilitator

Once birthparents and adoptive parents agree to have contact, the professional serves as a facilitator. This involves educating, counseling and mediating with the birthparents and the adoptive families. This is the phase when both parties are open to proceeding with some form of increased contact. Again, the goal of the professional is to help the families learn to manage their relationship on their own.

Those professionals who are well versed in the dynamics of adoption, can assist adoptive parents and birthparents in a sensitive manner. As mediators, they listen to the voices of those concerned, helping them to work out their agreements and disagreements. A facilitator has given up the traditional controls found in the world of adoption. The decision makers are the two families joined by the ties of adoption. Perhaps this is the normalizing of adoption.

Questions to ask when looking for a professional.

1. What is your philosophy on open adoption?

2. What are your beliefs about opening up adoptions of minor children?

3. What do you see as the benefits of opening up an adoption?

4. What do you see as the problems?

5. Have you had any experience in doing this kind of work before? If so, what was your role? Do you help locate individuals? Act as an intermediary? Provide counseling on contact issues?

6. Who have your primary clients been in your adoption work? (Birthparents? Adoptive parents, Adopted persons?)

7. What are your credentials? (Degrees, continuing education, professional involvements.)

8. What are your fees?

Where To Find A Professional To Work With

Organizations
The following groups can provide you with referrals to professionals in your area who act as intermediaries and facilitators.

American Association of Open Adoption Agencies
Visit their web site at http://www.openadoption.org/~bbetzen/ or call Jim Gritter at 616-947-8110.

National Adoption Information Clearinghouse
Visit their web site at http://www.calib.com/naic or call toll free (888) 251-0075.

Concerned United Birthparents
Provides assistance with search and reunion. Contact them at 2000 Walker Street, Des Moines, Iowa 50317. They also have a number of local support groups.

The Adoption Reconnection Directory by Curry Wolfe
Includes listings of intermediaries and facilitators as well as search and support groups. Contact her at: PO Box 230643, Encinitas, CA 92023-0643, telephone 760-753-8288, email ccwolfe@worldnet.att.net.

Professionals
Many agencies that practice open adoption are also willing to help individuals open semi-open and closed adoptions. In addition to these agencies, there are also a number of professionals in counseling practices that specialize in adoption. The following is a short listing. Some listed do not do search work but are willing to make the initial contact.

Adoption Counseling and Search
Patricia Dorner
206 Lochaven
San Antonio, TX 78213.
210-341-2070

Association of Open Adoption Agencies
Jim Gritter, Catholic Human Services
1000 Hasting
Traverse City, MI 49684
616-947-8110.

Center For Family Connections
P.O. Box 383246
Cambridge, MA 02238
617-547-0909

Kinship Center
Sharon Kaplan-Roszia
507 E. First Street, Suite D
Tustin, CA 92780
714-544-7646

Life Matters
Carol Demuth, MSW
5025 N. Central Expressway, Suite 3040
Dallas, TX 75205-3447
214-361-0055

Randolph Severson, PhD
5025 N. Central, Suite 3040, Dallas, TX 75205
214-521-4560

Chapter 4

The Preparation Process for Birthparents

As birthparents prepare themselves for contact with their children, there is a revisiting of the time of the pregnancy and the adoption. They report remembering how it felt to discover the pregnancy, the reactions of their parents, the treatment in the delivery room, and more. Flashing back to that period is usually accompanied by an intensity of emotion as fresh as the original experience. For many, the emotions have been deeply suppressed and allowing them to show themselves can be overwhelming. Yet, when birthparents allow themselves to feel their grief and loss, they report a healing process.

Birthparents often say they were emotionally "frozen in time" as a result of the adoption. What this means is, that though they do grow up and do adult things, there is a part of them that is glued to their age at the time of the adoption. This interferes with their ability to fully assume their adult roles with confidence and strength. The process of reconnecting with the child they placed for adoption allows for movement towards healing of the heart and spirit. The emotional intensity of reconnection cannot be denied. Being prepared for this and having the courage to let it happen, results in the strengthening and healing of birthparents. Stronger adults emerge who are better able to manage their lives.

Simultaneously, then, birthparents deal with their emotions regarding the adoption as well as all the on-going realities in their lives. This will include dealing with one's spouse, children, extended relatives and friends. Navigating each one of these areas also carries with it the opportunity to come out of the closet and to deal with issues within the family structure. The more thought that is given to situations that may arise, the more comfortably these will be handled.

Grieving

It is important that birthparents reflect on the years that have passed and can't be recovered. This is painful because it requires facing how huge the loss is. This is not to say that the feelings of loss have not been there before this. However, the reality and presence of the children adds another dimension to the experience. This is the case even when birthparents feel that the adoption was, and is, a good decision. Visualizing the growing child helps birthparents deal with whatever age the child is now. It is difficult to deal with a child who is well beyond the stage of infancy when the emotional picture many birthparents carry is that of a newborn. It will be helpful to prepare for the grief that usually surfaces.

The loss of the parenting role also has to be confronted. Birthparents by now are often raising subsequent children and know the joys and challenges of parenthood. They often reflect on how it might have been if they had raised their birthchild. The benefit of facing the emotions that arise is that they begin to absorb their truth at yet another level and continue the healing. It is important not to oversimplify this process. It does not happen as a one-time event, but rather over time.

Seeing the adopted child in the flesh is very emotional for birthparents. Even receiving pictures for the first time is so profound an emotional experience that it requires tremendous strength to look at them. Birthparents will often express confusion about the vast number of emotions they feel simultaneously: sadness, joy, anticipation, anger, fear etc. I want to emphasize that this is normal and part of the reconnection process.

The first meetings in person are very intense for everyone. Being able to physically see the child and his adoptive parents as a family, is both painful and reassuring for a birthparent. It is yet another opportunity to reflect on the adoption decision. We would be naive to think that regret is absent from these experiences. Yet, by facing the present, some level of resolution has a chance to occur. For many, it is a confirmation of the decision and an opportunity to move forward with a greater acceptance of the adoption.

Anticipating the children's range of behavior helps birthparents examine their own expectations. Some children are very comfortable with a hug of greeting while others stand back until some later time. Some children cling to their parents' side and yet others may go off and play, separating themselves from everyone. Allowing room for all these behaviors is recommended as this is how children manage levels of stress and anxiety. It is wise to be guided by the children's cues. The more informal the visit, the easier it tends to be. This may include a visit to a park or other outdoor area that still allows some time for privacy from crowds.

The good-byes at this early stage can be particularly difficult, especially because the relationship is still in the early stages and there can be a lot of uncertainty. Birthparents report that saying goodbye after a visit carries with it the memory of the original separation from the child. This is coupled with the fear of losing the child yet one more time if things do not work out well in the relationship. What birthparents need to remember is that, over time, the anguish they feel will diminish as they become assured of continued contact and visits. It is important, however, to acknowledge that there is an emotional risk in opening one's heart without a guarantee of what may be ahead.

In the early stages of getting acquainted, there is often a high degree of uncertainty about the frequency of contact. When silence occurs for a period of time, the belief often is that contact is no longer desired. Therefore, it is important for everyone involved to learn to communicate in ways that are as clear as possible. For this reason, it is recommended that the adults have an opportunity to speak on the phone and meet prior to including the children in these activities. This gives them a chance to discuss issues that may arise and how they think their relationship will develop. This will also be helpful as they figure out each person's role in the two families.

Another area of consideration is what birthparents will be called by their children. The usual pattern seems to be a first name alternately used with a title such as Mom or Dad. Though birthparents are pleased to be addressed in either manner, they often don't allow themselves the right to the parental titles. There are birthparents who candidly express the hope that their children will feel comfortable with mom and dad vocabulary. At the same time, the vast majority are very well aware of how loaded these words are and are perfectly happy to be called by a first name. Most birthparents handle this carefully because they don't want to hurt the adoptive parents. In fact, both the birthparents and the adoptive parents need to feel comfortable with whatever the children call their birthparents. The bottom line is that children know who their parents are and will not be confused by using Mom or Dad when referring to their birthparents.

They also need to feel comfortable with what other members of the birthfamily will be called. For example, there are more sets of grandparents, aunts, uncles, and cousins entering the children's lives. Children know at an early age that these are their relatives too. Whether they are allowed to claim them in that way will depend on the adults in their lives. This is especially true with adoptive parents who may not feel comfortable with family-type titles.

The timing for telling others

When birthparents look at what is at work in deciding who to tell about the adoption, they begin to deal with the difference between secrecy and privacy. Secrecy tends to be a major part of why people don't tell others about their involvement with adoption. Secrecy tends to carry shame by its side. We have learned from birthparents that shame is a major part of the birthparent experience. It includes the shame of the circumstances surrounding the pregnancy and the subsequent separation from one's own flesh and blood. Privacy has more to do with the choices one makes about personal matters that may not be anyone else's business, and therefore, are not shared. As contact occurs, secrecy often gets replaced with optional privacy; one can choose whom to tell about the adoption. The feelings attached to the adoption become less shameful and may disappear altogether.

Dealing with one's immediate family

When the birthparents' spouse is not aware of the adopted child, there is often an uncertainty about how to reveal the adoption. Birthparents are aware that their spouse may feel betrayed because such important information has been withheld. The greatest fear expressed by birthparents is that of losing the relationship with their spouse and/ or their children.

In my work, I have found that mates usually are accepting of the news though there is usually an adjustment period. Some of the struggles for the spouse revolve around the awareness that there was intimacy with another partner. The child is the physical proof of this. The fear that there may still be feelings for the other birthparent also figures in this. Concern about how the children born within the marriage will react, is also often expressed by the spouse. When a spouse is willing, using a professional can be helpful in working through these many issues.

Birthparents also struggle with whether to even tell the children they are raising about the adopted child. It is important that each birthparent decide whether to tell, and if so, when. In my experience, most do share with their children and find that they are excited about the prospect of another sibling entering the family picture. Sometimes there is an adjustment period that may include anger that the information was not shared before. For the most part though, the news is well received. Nonetheless, birthparents are entitled to make these decisions in their own time. It gives them control in an area where they usually have had little control. That is, the adoption experience usually did not give birthparents a voice in how things would go.

Sometimes birthparents wait to tell their children until there is a clearer picture that the contact will be on-going. They don't want the children they are raising to risk hurt if contact breaks off. Thinking about how and when to tell the children also allows for an evaluation of how and when to tell others. This fact needs to be honored by all who surround birthparents.

Birth order is another issue that is affected by the inclusion of the adopted sibling. Awareness of this helps in being sensitive to the affected children. For example, the oldest child is often no longer the oldest. In many families, this is a position of status. Now, the family structure has to be rearranged so as to allow the adopted child a spot. There may also be jealousy because concentrated attention is going to the adopted child or because of feelings of vulnerability about one's place in mom's heart. Sibling rivalry is common in any household and will show up here as well. Spreading one's attention and affection can be quite wearying. At the same time it will have a familiar feel in any household where there is more than one child.

Children of birthparents sometimes do not understand why their adopted sibling can't just move in with them. Part of the work involves helping them understand the permanence of adoption and the permanence of the families they are in. Young children, in particular, worry that since one child is already in a different family, the same fate may await them at some point. It takes some on-going communication to reassure the children of birthparents that this will not be the case. Birthparents are encouraged to anticipate their children's concerns and say the reassuring words even before any worries are expressed by their children.

Dealing with their own parents

During the course of opening an adoption, birthparents find themselves looking at their lives and the many ways the adoption has affected them. They often realize that their relationship and communication with their own parents were deeply affected. From the perspective of adulthood, many observe how their own parent-child ties have often suffered. The vast majority will say that the topic of adoption has been totally suppressed within their families.

Changing times, attitudes, and practices often give birthparents the courage to bring up the past. Old wounds are allowed to heal as communication can occur in a more tolerant world. Their parents will often confess that they too have suffered, wondering if they did the right thing by pressing for the adoption to happen. They state their silence was often guided by a fear of hurting their children or stirring emotions that were in check.

Needless to say, there are parents of birthparents who are not willing to deal with the adoption. They may still feel shame that a child was born under unacceptable circumstances. They may feel responsible for the anguish of their child and not be able to deal with it or the blame that anyone may direct at them. Sometimes these parents feel they failed as parents because the whole situation even happened—the sexual activity, the pregnancy, and the need for an adoption. It is important to recognize that these parents lost the opportunity to be grandparents to the adopted child. The inability to deal with the grief of this loss also sometimes keeps some from communicating in any way about the adoption.

When birthparents and their parents have an opportunity to air adoption issues, there can be a healing in their relationship. While most birthparents would like the blessing of their parents in opening the adoption, ultimately their first priority should be to do what they feel is best.

Under any circumstances, it can be very helpful if birthparents think about the time period surrounding the adoption and how their parents might have felt at the time. This review often happens when birthparents are themselves parents and often leads to one of the avenues in the healing process—forgiveness. They may have to forgive their parents for their inadequacies, their harsh judgment or whatever else that hurt them. This is not to say that all birthparents blame their parents for the adoption, but many do. Letting go of the anger and blame directed at their parents is an important part of the process. Interwoven in this is the self-blaming that birthparents often do. They may ask themselves why they didn't stand up to their parents? Why didn't they stand up to society? Why weren't they stronger? Older? Wealthier? The fact is they did the best they could and beating themselves up does not change that the adoption took place. Coming to terms with each part of the whole picture is what the healing process is about.

There are birthparents whose families have acknowledged the child through the years and allowed for discussion of the child's reality. These birthparents have felt supported and this eased their journey. The parent-child bond is usually strengthened by this.

When birthparents' parents are unaware of the adoption

There are situations where birthparents have never told their parents about the adoption. The opening of the adoption is an opportunity to tell them. As issues are faced, telling parents features as one significant area.

As with an unknowing spouse, the fear of judgment and rejection weighs heavily for birthparents. Many birthparents in this situation have made the observation that their parents have a way of reducing them to a child-like state. They describe family scenes where their parents demand to be in charge as they were during their childhood. There are parents who have a difficult time honoring the adult status of their children especially in areas that are emotionally charged. Therefore, it is wise to wait until they feel strong before they break the news to their parents.

Kirsten and her adoptive family established contact with both her birthparents when Kirsten was a small child. Her birthfather's parents were not aware of her existence. When she was a teenager, her birthfather felt ready to tell his parents about his child. They were thrilled to welcome her to the family fold. Who knows what might have happened had they been told before. There is no way to recapture lost time. Her birthfather's wishes for determining the timing of this sharing was respected by Kirsten's family. The relationship is evolving as Kirsten incorporates her newly found set of grandparents.

Her family has observed that the grandparents have been very excited to welcome her. To demonstrate this they have showered her with treats when she visits. Kirsten seems to be handling this well and her parents are very comfortable with the gift giving. For some, this can be threatening. Too much gift giving can get in the way of the relationship. In this particular case, it is working well. Each family has its own comfort zone for this kind of generosity. It can especially be uncomfortable if the birthfamily is better off than the adoptive family. This has to do with parents wanting to provide in all ways for their children and feeling vulnerable when someone is more financially able. Here too, communication between the two families about what is acceptable is crucial. These grandparents want to shower her with gifts and love while they have a chance. Kirsten and her parents understand this.

Grandparents today are usually more receptive of the news, especially when their children are well into their adulthood. Our society is also more accepting of children born without marriage. While there are those who have major concerns about what the neighbors will think, there are also ones who feel sadness that they weren't there for their children. Their emotions also get intermingled with the sadness of a grandchild growing up outside of the family and the gratefulness to be a part of his life now.

Not all grandparents react positively to the news. That is why revealing this information is best done when there is a sense of personal strength which can sustain whatever the reaction.

Extended birthfamily considerations

There is a ripple effect when adoptions are opened. Not only does it affect birthparents and their immediate family, but it also affects extended family members. The reception of family members can range from totally supportive to non-accepting. Birthparents need to be clear with extended family members about what behavior they will and will not accept.

I have learned that extended family members of birthparents often deal with the same issues as the birthparents themselves. Besides the parents of birthparents, others who are affected include siblings, grandparents, aunts, uncles, and cousins. Being included can offer them an opportunity for expressing and dealing with their emotions. For example, siblings may feel guilty for not having kept the adopted child within the family, even when age and capability would have prevented this. Having an opportunity to welcome the adopted person to the family fold is healing.

Sometimes birthparents don't wish to allow their family members any contact with the adopted child. In some cases, it has to do with their resentment that the needed help, so that the child could have stayed within the family, was not offered at the time of the adoption. On occasion, birthparents block contact, fearing that their relatives will be too overwhelming for the adoptive family. They are afraid that the adoptive parents may just withdraw and not deal with anyone, including them.

An added complexity is that while children may focus on and welcome birthparents into their lives, they are not always as inclusive of extended family members. Over time, this tends to shift but, at the early stages, enthused relatives may feel thwarted and rejected.

There are also adoptive parents who, for a variety of reasons, may have no interest in the extended family. Usually, it has to do with identifying the birthparents as the focal point of contact. As the relationship between the birthparents and adoptive parents grows, other birthfamily members very often enter the picture. For example, if the adopted child's birthday celebration is being shared, with time, cousins, aunts, and uncles may attend.

A focus on birthfathers

The inclusion of birthfathers in the opening of adoptions is a natural one because they are also a part of the child's birthfamily. While adoptive parents usually start with a focus on the birthmother's side of the family, eventually efforts are made to also contact the birthfather. There are birthmothers who are very opposed to including birthfathers in any part of the adoption. They frequently express a deep hurt that, during the pregnancy and adoption process, the birthfather abandoned them. Therefore, they feel these men do not deserve to be in touch with their children ever again. A lifetime of punishment is their sentence. It is important to acknowledge the pain experienced by birthmothers. However, no matter what the relationship is or was between the birthparents, an adopted child's reality is that he has a birthmother and a birthfather.

It is also important to pay attention to what has been learned from adopted adults who have searched for their birthfamilies. Their message is that they want the full truth and that includes making contact with the birthfathers.

Time is fluid and as people grow up they frequently assume responsibility for behaviors from their youth. This is often the case with birthfathers. To put them in eternal punishment, in order to help birthmothers get revenge, is not constructive for anyone. If the birthmothers need to hang onto their rage, that is their choice. However the adopted person and the adoptive parents can make other choices and decisions.

Sometimes birthmothers discourage contact with the birthfather because they are fearful that contact will be refused. Trying to spare their children from hurt is certainly understandable. At the same time, one will never know the outcome of any action if one doesn't try. The adoptive parent of minors assess this risk each step of the way, just as adopted adults do it during their searches.

There are birthfathers who actively participated during the pregnancy in a supportive manner and acknowledged their paternity. The men who acknowledged their roles are the easiest to approach. This is a good time to verify the identity of the named birthfather. There will be a percentage of cases where he was incorrectly identified by the birthmother in order to protect or exclude the correct one. While the majority of cases do not fall into this situation, it is wise to obtain the verification from the birthmother. It has been my experience that caution is indicated.

An example of this involved a paternal grandmother who had stayed in touch with the placing agency. An inquiry by the adoptive mother of the now 14 year old adopted boy led to letter writing. An exchange of pictures created a concern that this might be an incorrectly named birthfather. The candid exploration of this led to a search for the birthmother. She did not respond. Here was a willing birthfather now presented with a dilemma that the child he had carried within might not be his. In the absence of the birthmother's participation, a DNA test would be possible. This, however, is a costly procedure both financially and emotionally.

A similar situation occurred when a birthmother, struggling with her own issues, confessed that the man she had named was not the right one. She asked that the agency personnel notify him of her deception. She had carried tremendous guilt about this misinformation and its ramifications. The agency felt an obligation to notify the birthfather of the misrepresentation to set the record straight. This very honorable man was very distraught as he had envisioned the growing up process of this child and hoped for a contact sometime in the future. He now had to deal with the grief of losing the child even more definitively.

The child was now 11 years old and asking a multitude of questions. His adoptive parents did what they could to respond to his need but would not allow a DNA test for fear of traumatizing him. Thus, the birthfather was left with the anguish and uncertainty of his assumed fatherhood with no way of knowing the truth. The child was left with a closed door as his birthmother could not face contact beyond one letter. She also refused to name the correct father.

We also must consider the birthfather who was excluded from the adoption process and didn't even know a child was born. This individual is often overwhelmed and may seek proof of his paternity. If the existence of the child is accepted and he participates, he will go through the multitude of feelings associated with adoption. For example, he will probably experience sadness for the lost years, anger for being excluded from the adoption decision and shame that he wasn't considered worthy of knowing about the child. Very often these men deal with their feelings on their own. Sometimes the birthmothers help them by sharing what they have learned and experienced. Those who are willing to seek outside help may fare better in the relationship with the child and the adoptive parents. This is because open adoption is a foreign experience for most people. When there is an opportunity to learn about it and how it affects all involved, the relationship with the adopted child and his adoptive parents will benefit.

Another situation often encountered is the birthfather who was notified at the time of the birth but denied paternity. In my experience, these birthfathers were often guided by the fear of the impending fatherhood and wish they had done things differently. These men are often grateful for the opportunity to respond now and enter into contact when it is offered. When this happens, it is quite usual for the birthmothers to be upset as they still often carry negative feelings about the birthfathers. Sometimes they don't want to share the child, feeling that these birthfathers are undeserving even now.

While the adoptive family may be understanding of the birthmother's feelings, it is not appropriate to shut a door of possibility. The child deserves access to both sides of his birthfamily when this is possible. As mentioned before, it does not mean that the birthmother and birthfather have to establish a new relationship with one another.

When the birthparents are married

When birthparents are married, there are some additional considerations. There are those couples who have, throughout their marriage, spoken of their missing child and thus, done some emotional work together. I have found, however, that a larger proportion tend to not discuss the adoption. Seldom are both partners at the same place emotionally. Therefore, contact with the child creates the opportunity for the couple to communicate more about the adoption and how this affected them. This frequently leads to increased healing for each person and for the couple.

This does not mean that this work is easy. There is so much to deal with: full siblings, the family that might have been, the guilt of a continued relationship excluding their child, the decision process at the time of the birth, and more. The revisiting of the past seems unavoidable and those couples who do not blame each other for the fact that the adoption happened, seem to do better.

There are those couples who are not in agreement about contact with the adoptive family. One partner may be ready to enter into the relationship and not the other. It is important that couples respect each other's wishes regarding whether there will be contact, and if so, how much. Some couples are able to manage the situation when just one spouse has contact. This can be very stressful, though, because it is such an emotional experience that involves them both.

Sometimes, the discomfort of one results in the withdrawal from contact of the other. Or, the active participant may bring in the unwilling partner over time. Giving each other space allows for different degrees of readiness and reduces marital conflict.

Each spouse will have his/her own way of managing the emotions related to the adoption. In our society, it is normal for women to show their feelings openly. Men tend to be more private, keeping major emotions under wraps. It may be hard for the birthmother to understand that, while she and her husband may be experiencing similar emotions, he is processing them differently. This can cause difficulties as each partner deals with the reentry of the child into their lives.

Married birthparents are sometimes intimidating to adoptive parents. This stems from the fear that somehow their child will be drawn to taking his place in the family where he would have grown up, had he not been adopted. When the birth and adoptive parents have an understanding of this sensitive issue, they are more likely to handle it with a caring awareness and feel safer in the relationship being established. There can be an honoring of the fact that the two adoptive parents and the two birthparents can cooperatively exist in the child's life.

Questions to ask yourself if you are a birthparent

1. Why do I want to open this adoption?
   - What led me to choose adoption for my child?
   - Why is this a good time to open the adoption?
   - What do I want to tell my child?
   - Should I contact the adoptive parents myself or should I use an intermediary?
   - Who can I use for preparation and support as contact occurs?

2. How am I dealing with the adoption?
   - What fantasies have I had about my child and his adoptive family?
   - Have I been able to study, work, marry and generally function as the years have passed?
   - How has my relationships with my spouse, family, and children been effected by the adoption?
   - Is the adoption the main focus of my life?
   - Do I hope contact with my child will solve my problems?
   - What are my feelings about the adoption? Do I feel it was the right choice for myself? For my child?
   - How do I feel about my child's other birthparent?
   - How do I feel about the adoptive parents of my child?

3. What do I expect from the opening of this adoption?
   - What part do I want to play in my child's life?
   - What relationship do I want with my child and his adoptive family?
   - What do I want my child to know about me and the adoption?
   - How would I handle a delay in getting to know my child?
   - What do I want my child to call me?
   - Am I ready for the roller coaster of emotions that are a part of having contact? What kind of preparation and support am I getting?
   - Could I handle it if the adoptive parents wanted contact with the other birthparent?
   - How would I handle learning that my child's life has been difficult? (i.e. divorced parents; emotional, learning or health problems)
   - What supports do I have in case the adoptive parents do not want contact now?

Chapter 5

Adoptive Parent Preparation

Adoptive parents are most often focused on their children's needs when trying to link up with the birthfamily. They are sometimes surprised by the emotions that surface for them as well. As contact evolves, adoptive parents benefit from examining the issues that affect them. This will include a heightened awareness of how their family was created. No matter how long their children have been a part of their lives, or how strong their relationships are, contact makes everything more real and more concrete. Part of this involves facing, in a different way, the fact that their children were born to real people who connect them to their genetic heritage. This is not to say they haven't faced or dealt with this truth before. Contact, however, creates a qualitative difference that can feel different and require some emotional work. In no way does this deny the strong bonds between the adoptive parents and their children. The truth is that, through adoption, the two families and their family trees have been joined, not separated. Sometimes it takes time for adoptive parents to reach a comfortable place which allows both families to feel real and welcomed.

Needless to say, infertility is recognized as a central issue for adoptive parents. The birthparents represent the couple who were able to create the child they couldn't. Just as the child represents the loss experienced by the birthparents, the birthparents represent the loss experienced by the adoptive parents. The birthparents are fertile, the adoptive parents are not. The other side of this coin is that the birthparents represent the realization of their dreams—parenthood. Through them, the long-awaited child entered their lives. The birthparents' loss was their gain.

Entitlement is another area that is significant for adoptive parents. It relates to the right to be the parents of the adopted child. The more adoptive parents feel comfortable about issues such as infertility, the more they are likely to feel entitled to be the child's parents.

Adoptive parents deal with entitlement whether they have learned the vocabulary or not. Many of their parenting decisions are influenced by how secure they are as parents by adoption. For example, discipline can be one area that is affected by these feelings. Sometimes adopted children are allowed more lax discipline because adoptive parents don't feel they have the right to set limits. Children need parents who are strong and set appropriate limits. The more entitled the parents feel, the stronger their parenting.

Where closed adoption supports exclusive rights to the child, the opening of contact promotes sharing. Again, the more secure the adoptive parents are, the more they are willing to share their children with birthparents. They also tend to be more comfortable in acknowledging the role the birthparents play in their lives.

Parent-child interaction

Sometimes it is difficult for adoptive parents to witness the excitement exhibited by their children at the prospect of contact with birthparents. Feelings of uncertainty, insecurity, jealousy and sadness can intermingle with the parents' genuine eagerness to have it happen. This, too, is normal. Eventually the feelings sort themselves out as the course of action becomes more familiar and relationships grow.

It is helpful to the children when parents communicate clearly with them as well. Children worry a great deal about how their parents are truly feeling about birthparent involvement. Sometimes, even in the face of very clear parental enthusiasm, the children exhibit uncertainty about their parents' comfort.

It is important for adoptive parents to learn about children's feelings and behaviors during the course of contact. When they are familiar with these, they are better able to help their children deal with whatever arises. Sometimes seeking professional help is indicated. For example, there is a tendency to want to protect parents from hurt, as well as a sometimes unconscious fear of losing them. It is not appropriate for children to assume the care of adults. Yet, some try by showing a diminished interest in the progress of birthparent contact as a way of covering up the fears mentioned. The adoptive parents may feel relief that the birthparents are not quite as needed as it previously appeared. Family ties will be strengthened when adoptive parents and their children build some skills in communicating clearly and honestly with one another. When families prepare themselves for contact, or use the services of a professional, considering possible scenarios is very helpful.

Crying, in particular, concerns children since they read the tears as distress. Parents are encouraged to label the emotions associated with the tears so that the children understand that it doesn't mean that they don't want to proceed with contact. Providing examples of times when we cry because of a swelling of emotion can be helpful. One typical example is the flow of tears at weddings when everyone is so obviously happy.

As the adoptive parents express their assurances to their children, another curve may come their way when children refer to birthparents as "my mom" and "my dad." Sometimes they don't understand the emotional connection the children feel to these birthparents from whom they have been separated for a lifetime. They ask themselves how the children can express loving thoughts and feelings without knowing these family members.

Feelings of vulnerability and of possibly losing the exclusivity associated with the role of parenthood often appear. Acknowledging these feelings permits adoptive parents to work through them. What becomes evident, as competition diminishes and relationships grow, is that the children are able to integrate all parents- both adoptive and birthparents. As in the search experience with adults, the bonds with adoptive parents are strengthened as the children feel validated by them.

Adoptive parents are encouraged to review their role as decisions are made about the steps that will be taken. It is appropriate for them to make parenting decisions about how the contact will evolve. They sometimes express a sense that they have to allow whatever the birthparent requests. Sometimes this comes out of guilt, insecurity or threatened entitlement. By being open about these areas, they will be better able to examine what is going on.

An example of this, would be determining at which point a young child might spend time alone with the birthfamily. It is a very different scenario to consider an overnight visit for a 17 year old versus a 7 year old. Using family rules for how permission is granted in these situations offers a useful guide.

This does not mean that birthparents have to be silent about what they hope will happen. Instead, it means respecting what is mutually comfortable, focusing on the child's welfare. A birthparent can extend an invitation to the adoptive parents that can be accepted when both parties are ready. It would be advisable for birthparents to make invitations to the adoptive parents. This way children are not put in the middle of conflicting ideas or plans. This also recognizes that the parents are the decision makers while the child is growing up.

Emily began to have contact with her birthmother when she was just a toddler. Years of visits (not including overnights) and other forms of contact built trust between the adoptive and birth families. Her birthmother eventually married and had another child. When Emily was 14, she went out of town to stay with her birthmother for a week.

This was a major step as she would be without her adoptive family. She also would be sharing time with the baby born to her birthmother. The visit allowed Emily to incorporate the baby as her sister and to emotionally process that her birthmother was mothering another child. Witnessing this bond between subsequent children and the birthmother can be difficult for the adopted child. Each emotional step taken, even when difficult, allows the adopted person to deal with the truth. Balancing a sense of belonging in both adoptive and birthfamilies takes time and emotional work. By being able to experience her birthmother up close, Emily had the opportunity to do some of this work. This will continue over time as she makes sense of her adoption with growing maturity and awareness.

Children have to have a clear sense that their parents will continue to be their parents even with the birthparent inclusion. They need to know that decisions made on their behalf are made whether parents are considering events with friends, aunts and uncles or any member of the birthfamily.

Extended adoptive family considerations
When children are adopted, they are claimed by extended adoptive family members as family. It is important that relatives from within the adoptive family consider the children genuine family by both their actions and their words. Adopted children are very sensitive to whether there is true acceptance of their belonging. The degree to which they feel they are part of the extended family will play a significant part in their emotional well-being.

When adoptions are opened, and the birthfamily comes into the picture, some relatives may fear being displaced by birthfamily. There may be comments about what right do "they" have after all, "they gave up their rights." These judgments are often a cover up for feelings of vulnerability. They may also include deeply held convictions about how adoption should work. Ultimately, however, the decision makers are the adoptive parents, birthparents, and adopted children.

There are a number of ways to address difficult relatives including discussion and education. Addressing the fear of losing these children to the birthfamily may pave the way to constructive communication. When families are able to share their children and welcome all significant bonds, everyone has an opportunity to be confirmed.

There are families who welcome birthfamily even when it means changing the original rules. Birthparents are sometimes overwhelmed by the love they feel from adoptive families. Finding acceptance instead of judgment provides the potential for healing. Finding appreciation for giving life and creating a family can be bittersweet. The acknowledged sacrifice may unleash a grief that is free to flow. Relatives from the adoptive family may have a difficult time witnessing the grief that paved the way to their joy. Expecting the birthparents to react with unbridled happiness when the contact becomes possible, they are often taken by surprise by the range of emotions they witness. After all, the message had been that birthparents forgot, put the experience behind them, and went on with their lives. Learning about each other's experiences builds empathy and a new understanding. If each member is open to learn and experience with an open heart, both families will be enriched. This too, may take time— the ingredient that fuels, nurtures and defines relationships.

Questions to ask yourself if you are an adoptive parent.

1. Why do I want to open the adoption?
   - What led me to choose adoption to become a parent?
   - Why is this a good time to open the adoption?
   - Am I opening it because I am anticipating my child's need to know or because my child has asked for information and contact?
   - Am I comfortable with the contact or am I doing it reluctantly?
   - What are my fantasies about the birthparents?
   - How do I see my role in establishing and maintaining contact with the birthparents?
   - What part do I want the birthparents to play in our family?
   - Should contact be made directly by us or should we use an intermediary?
   - Who can we use for preparation and support as the contact occurs?

2. How am I dealing with the adoption?
   - If infertility was a reason for the adoption, how am I coping with the fact that I am (was) infertile?
   - How comfortable am I talking about adoption with my child and others?
   - Do I feel entitled to be my child's parent and make parenting decisions on his or her behalf?
   - What are my feelings toward my child's birthparents?

3. What expectations do I have about opening the adoption?
   - What part do I expect to play in the birthparents' lives?
   - Am I comfortable learning more about the birthparents? For example, are they doing well or is their life difficult? Do we have a lot in common or are the two families very different?
   - What relationship do I want with the birthparents?
   - What do I want the birthparents to know about our family?
   - How will I decide when my child is ready for each step of the contact (letters, telephone calls, meeting for the first time, meeting over the years)?

- Am I able to see my child being affectionate with his or her birthparents?
- Am I able to share my child with his birthparents?
- Do I think or hope that opening the adoption will solve my child's problems? Do I see this as a cure-all?
- What supports does our family have in case the birthparents are not open to contact?

Chapter 6

Preparing the Adopted Child

When opening adoptions with infants, toddlers, and preschoolers (ages 0 – 5), it is really the adoptive parents who must be well prepared. The younger the child, the less elaborate the preparation is. It is helpful to examine the many issues that can arise and how they can be handled so as to make the contact as smooth as possible.

Sometimes, with this age group, parents express concern about how to introduce birthparents, wondering if it would be desirable to use less "loaded" vocabulary. Even small children, however, can learn correct birthparent related vocabulary and begin to understand the meaning behind the words. Under no circumstances would it be recommended to misrepresent the identity of birthfamily. For example, sometimes birthparents are introduced as aunts, uncles, or family friends. Usually this is done with the hope that the children will not be confused by the titles birthmother and birthfather.

Unfortunately, what starts out as an effort to help the child ends up being an untruth that is hard to correct. It also serves no constructive purpose. It is much easier to build on the truth of who these people are than to have to make sense of a new identity for them later on. To think of someone as an aunt and then discover that she is really one's birthmother requires a big emotional leap. Even when an aunt is very loved and special, the issues are totally different than when a person is actually a birthmother.

Another aspect of this involves communication in the family. Preschool children frequently ask questions about their birthparents. They want to know what their names are and what they look like. When these birthparents are already in their lives, but misidentified, the adoptive parents must cover this up. It also requires that the birthparents be part of the cover-up. When the truth comes out, the child's ability to trust all his parents will probably be affected. It is therefore wiser to wait to schedule the visit until everyone is comfortable with identifying the birthparent correctly.

Once a visit is planned, it is a good idea to tell the child so that he is not taken by surprise when it happens. Once the time is set, however, it is best if there is not a big time delay. The reason for this is that the concept of time is difficult for a young child to grasp. A few hours may feel like a lifetime to them. It is sufficient to tell a child in this age group a day or two before the visit. This way, questions and feelings that may come up can be dealt with before the visit.

It is hard for a child to imagine how the visit will go, so, walking through it beforehand is helpful. For example, he can be told where they are going to get together, what they might do, how he might feel, and about how long the visit will be.

The conversation might go like this: "We're going to get together with Jill tomorrow afternoon at Jolly Park. Mommy and Daddy will be there with you. You'll have a chance to meet Jill and even play with her if you want to. Maybe you'll want to hug her when you see her. If you do, go ahead. If you don't, that's O.K., too. We want you to be comfortable. We really love her and are excited about meeting her. We will probably stay together for about and hour and a half. That's about as long as Sesame Street and Mr. Rogers. What do you think? And I want you to know that when we're done visiting, you, Mommy, and Daddy will come home together. Sometimes kids get nervous, and it's better if we talk about it. Let me know if you have any questions, O.K.?"

The message should be tailored to the child's age and attention span. It may be that just a few comments are communicated at a time if the child seems to be tuning out. It is a good idea to go over this information again the day of the visit to refresh his memory. The goal is to make the visit as tension-free as possible.

Another area that needs to be considered in the location of the visit. Children often feel confined in a formal setting, so it is a good idea to consider meeting at a park or a place where the child can move around freely. Some adoptive parents feel comfortable having the visit at their home, which does involve bringing the birthparent more intimately into their world. This may come naturally since there has usually been a fair amount of prior contact through letters and phone calls. Being at home allows the child to roam in a safe and familiar place. The bottom line is to choose a place where the child and the adults can be at ease. The length of the visit also deserves some thought and planning. Being flexible is wise. Some children can handle a few hours of relaxed visiting while others may be more comfortable with a shorter visit. The adoptive parents need to evaluate how the child seems to be doing because they know how the child responds in many different situations. If a professional is involved, he can also have input.

During the visit, the focus is on observing how the child appears to be handling all that is going on. For example, if the child is clinging to his adoptive mother, he may be very anxious and need some reassurance. Young children usually need time to warm up to new adults, so it is important to pay attention to what appears to be comfortable for the child. One way to break the ice is to have toys that the child can play with. As time passes, he may allow the birthparent to play, too. The idea is not to crowd him or expect him to perform for the birthparent. The more free-flowing the visit is, the better it tends to work out.

It is a good idea to talk with the child briefly after the visit to evaluate how he is dealing with it. Young children do not usually get into long conversations. They may say, "It was fun," "She is pretty," or "It was OK." They may talk about it more later. The main focus of these conversations is to build some familiarity with the birthparent so the child feels comfortable during each visit.

The school age child - ages 6-12

As the child enters the school years, more preparation is usually possible. This is a good time to involve a professional who can help the child and the family get ready for whatever may arise. It is appropriate to tell the child that an effort is being made to locate his birthparents. Sometimes adoptive parents hesitate to do this because they are afraid of hurting the child if the birthparent won't participate. Telling the child about the search, conveys to him that his questions and needs are being responded to. This does not eliminate the possibility of hurt if contact is not possible, but it is guided by the truth. Preparing him for that risk is advised while also telling him that most birthparents do accept the invitation. Helping him understand why birthparents don't come forth, lowers the chance that the child will assume it is because he's not worthy of their love.

Children in this age group have a greater attention span and are more able to talk about the experience. Some time can be spent talking about fantasies, and questions children have, and the many ways he will get to know his birthparent. Keeping the conversation simple and fairly brief works quite well with the younger children. The older children will be able to handle more discussion and take in more information. When a professional is used, the adoptive parents join in. The idea is to recognize that this is a family venture, and everyone needs to think about what is ahead. When a professional is not used, the parents are the ones who would cover these areas.

Some of the fantasies children have are about going to live with the birthmother. Because they don't yet understand the permanence of the adoption, they may think that contact is the first step towards going to live with her. This can be both a pleasant thought and a scary one. The child can be told that the plan is to get to know one another, but that everyone goes to his own home afterwards.

As children get older, they also wonder what it would have been like to live with their birthparents. Some of them believe that life would be perfect if only they could be with their perfect birthparents. This is very normal and may bring out some mourning about what might have been. The children may be sad and even cry. They may also feel and show anger about the adoption. This is another way that grief shows itself. Letting them know that sometimes children feel happy, angry, and sad prepares them for these possibilities.

Adopted children have an unending list of questions about their birthfamilies and their adoption. Some of these are spoken and some are kept private. The open adoption experience usually helps them feel more comfortable about having and asking questions. It is important to know that every question is significant to the child. Every question that gets answered removes some of the mystery that has usually surrounded the adoption. Usually, children ask who they look like and why they were adopted. They also often request pictures, usually of their birthmothers.

Children tend to be impatient and often cannot understand why they must wait to see their birthparents. It is important to discuss the ways they will get to know their birthparent. This includes letter writing, talking on the phone, and eventually meeting one another. It is not unusual for this process to take six months to a year. Taking time to get acquainted improves the chances of a long-term relationship. The emotions and issues of making contact are so intense that allowing everyone time to deal with them makes them more manageable. This, in turn, helps the connection be more stable.

Some children want to keep their letters and pictures private, even from their parents. This should be respected unless there is a concern about content. The value of an intermediary is that, usually, letters are screened for content and appropriateness in all directions. This is done to assist the families as they work on the foundation of their relationship. Families who do this on their own will have to make decisions about giving privacy to children. That is why the trust among the adults is so vital.

As much as everyone may seem ready to move on with getting acquainted, there are sometimes long delays in answering letters. Sometimes there is no response at all. This delay is hurtful and tends to create anger, hurt, and disappointment. When children are the ones waiting, helping them understand why a birthparent may not be responding may ease the pain. Even so, most children experience the birthparent's silence as another rejection. Children do not understand that writing is difficult for the birthparents. When birthparents are slow to respond, it is fine to write the birthparent again, explaining that even a short letter can carry a child for a long time. It is important to a child to be acknowledged.

Sally, a birthmother, and the family of her daughter were very excited to pursue contact after many years of nothing. They both had come forward inquiring about each other at the agency where the closed adoption happened. Both were notified of the mutual interest. Letters and pictures promptly arrived from the adoptive mom and the adopted girl. Sally was overjoyed to receive them. Then there was silence.

As time passed, the concerned adoptive mother called to say her daughter was feeling hurt that there had been no timely answer. Sally said she felt paralyzed with the emotions that surged through her. She needed time to feel them and begin to deal with them. While the daughter still felt her own hurt and disappointment, Sally needed the time she asked for to get into balance within herself.

Another delay factor affecting all parties is the desire to write the perfect letter. It is more important to send a letter than to take forever writing and rewriting it. Being aware of what the children want to hear can help in writing the letter. It is helpful to think about what the child might like to hear. It is also useful to treat letter writing as though it were intended for a friend or penpal.

Children enjoy hearing about favorite colors, foods, music, and what the birthparent likes to do. They are also interested in knowing about pets, brothers and sisters. Being told that they are loved and remembered is very important to them. Early letters do not need to go into deep explanations as to why the adoption took place. It may be more appropriate to be gentle and brief about this subject. The letters children write tend to include the subject areas they want to hear about as well. So it is typical for them to share their favorites in many categories. They often will write about their teachers, best friends, and family.

In this age group and older, children may be jealous of birthsiblings who have had the birthparent in their lives. The child might say that he is sad that he is not living with his brothers and sisters or that his birthsiblings are lucky because they are with the birthparent. Sometimes, the child wonders what he did wrong that made the birthmother put him in another family. He may also express anger that she was able to raise the other children but not him.

This is a normal grief reaction and does not mean that the child wants to move in with the birthparents. When adoptive parents express empathy for these feelings, the child feels validated. It doesn't take away the hurt, but it does allow the child to express himself. They might say something as brief as, "I understand how you are feeling. I'm here to be with you and talk about it with you." It is often hard for a child to understand that the birthmother did the best she could at the time she made the decision. A major outcome of making contact is that the child will have the opportunity to hear the story of his adoption from his birthmother. Seeing her emotions and hearing the words helps the child handle his emotions. As relationships build, the focus on building sibling ties grows and jealousy tends to diminish.

After a period of letter writing to get acquainted, the contact may move to adult directed telephone calls and then to visits. It is helpful to children when they can walk through what is expected to happen with each step that is taken. For example, a phone call may flow more smoothly if the child thinks ahead of some questions he would like to ask or topics he would like to discuss. Parents standing by to assist, especially at the earlier stages, offer visible support for the call. It doesn't mean they have to hear every word spoken but can slip in if the child seems to want or need this. It is not unusual for young children to want their parents to be there. They usually don't carry on prolonged conversations like teens do.

By the time visits are scheduled, there should be some level of familiarity between the adoptive and birthfamilies. Even so, every step is a big one. Seeing each other in the flesh makes each person real in a very intense way. Preparing children for emotions they may feel or witness, is a good idea. Giving them tools for letting their parents know if they wish to end the visit before the planned time reduces stress of the unknown. Keeping the first visits relatively short is a good idea with this age group as well. One or two hours may be the limit for the child.

It is not unusual for children to demonstrate great enthusiasm one moment and not much at all in the next. This is why it is the task of the adults to commit to the relationship. Children developmentally may not stay focused for very long. This does not diminish the importance of building relationships over time. We can compare this to how they handle grandparents and other relatives. They love them and enjoy their presence but giving them attention may be intermittent. This does not make them any less important in the children's lives. Instead, this is a normal pattern of behavior.

By beginning the ties with birthfamily while the children are young, adoption issues are addressed gradually by everyone involved. Though issues don't go away, the likelihood that they will be faced and worked through increases.

Preparing adolescents

Adolescence is a time of beginning emancipation. Parental involvement in all areas is certainly appropriate, but the loosening of the ties is natural. How does one handle the integration of birthfamily during this stage of development? Honoring the family while giving the adolescent a voice is admittedly a delicate process.

Sometimes this age group wants to connect with birthparents without the involvement of the adoptive parents. One way to handle this is to strike a balance so that there is time for everyone to be together and time when the teen and birthparent can be alone.

Both sets of parents must trust one another and support each other in a unified manner. Adoptive parents need to feel that the birthparents will honor their family and uphold family rules and values.

Birthparents need to feel that they have an important ongoing role in the child's life even though they are not parenting. When trust exists, the need to be vigilant diminishes and the parents feel less vulnerable.

The Nickson family contacted the birthmother of their daughter, Kari, when Kari was 14-1/2 years old. The reason they wanted to do this was that Kari had many questions about her adoption. They used a professional to help them with all the stages of the contact.

Lita, the birthmother, was delighted to be contacted. She had always felt that adoption was the right decision for her child and had thought about her through the years wondering how she was doing. Lita was open to having whatever contact Kari and her adoptive parents were comfortable with.

After more than a year of intermittent letter writing, it appeared that there might be a meeting. As the time approached, however, it was obvious that Kari was not ready for it. She was involved with may activities and her focus was not on meeting Lita. Neither Lita nor Kari's parents wanted to press her in any way. Kari said she was satisfied with the letters she had received so far and seemed to have no further need to be in touch at the time. She was open to continue receiving mail from Lita if Lita wanted to continue writing. Always respectful, Lita let Kari lead the way. She wrote a few times and was careful not to pressure Kari.

Another year passed before Kari was ready to correspond more regularly again. This time, Lita and Kari's parents spoke on the phone. The adults were comfortable with one another and trusted one another. Even though they asked Kari if she would like to talk on the phone with Lita, she still did not feel comfortable or ready. She said that she had a lot going on in her life and didn't have time to deal with a more intense relationship. Lita always respected her wishes, they continued corresponding for a few more months.

When Lita had a business trip to the area where the Nicksons lived, she asked if the Nicksons and Kari wanted to spend some time with her. She extended the invitation in a very gentle way so that no one would feel pressured. Almost immediately, Kari decided she was ready. She said she really preferred to meet Kari in person rather than talk on the telephone.

Everyone gave Kari a major voice in how the visit would go. Since the parents were comfortable with Lita, they knew that if Kari were to spend time alone with Lita that it would be just fine. Kari said she wanted Lita to come to their home so that everyone could be together. At first, she thought that she would share most of the time with her parents. As it turned out, the visit did start out in the Nickson's home and then Lita and Kari went out on their own.

Kari's parents were very supportive of the relationship with Lita. There was a genuine fondness and respect between Lita and Kari's parents. They had laid a good foundation by taking their time in getting acquainted and building trust.

With younger children, the management of the relationship is more in adult hands, but with teens, the level of their commitment plays a bigger role. It is important to take into account their need and ability to participate. However, they also need to be sensitive to the feelings of birthparents. It is difficult in both directions if contact is established and then interrupted because of unequal needs.

As with younger children, it is valuable to spend some time getting acquainted through correspondence. Teenagers may be resistant to this as immediate gratification is so typical in this age group. Additionally, long-term thinking is not well developed. Being in a hurry to meet does not help build an enduring relationship. Instead, it tends to sabotage it.

The value of taking the time to get acquainted often gets acknowledged after the fact when everyone understands how intense the experience is. We are not talking here about prolonging the process indefinitely. However, allowing some time helps everybody deal with the intensity of the situation, making it less overwhelming. The time taken to exchange letters serves an important purpose. It allows everyone to maintain some distance while dealing with the emotions. It is more intense to talk on the telephone and even more intense to meet in person. Letter writing helps build up to the actual meeting.

Even the first exchange of letters and pictures are very emotional for adopted children, adoptive parents, and birthparents. Even pre-schoolers are touched when they get a letter or a picture from a birthparent.

As the teen and the birthparent get to know one another through letters, sometimes one person writes more letters than another. Sometimes, too many letters arriving too frequently can be overwhelming and interfere with the relationship.

Each type of contact gives a sense of how the relationship will evolve. If one person is too suffocating or too desperate, it can scare off the person who is on the receiving end. In this situation, clear and honest communication is important. It is better to say, "This is too much pressure for me. Let's find what we're both comfortable with" than to shut the door completely.

It is not unusual for the letter-writing stage to last four to eight months. During this time, three or four letters may be exchanged. Even when there is a real desire to know each other, people tend to take their time between letters. Each of the parties has a life outside of the adoption, and there is only so much time available. If one person is a better letter writer than the other, it is OK to write before an answer is received. Remember, though to keep it pleasant and not suffocating. Finding a balance is what is important.

After some time, most adoptive families and birthparents feel ready to phone one another. In most situations, it is a natural step because everyone feels less nervous about being in touch. Small children typically chat briefly, but it is not unusual for a teen to enjoy very lengthy conversations. This is especially the case with the first few conversations when there is so much to learn about one another. For teenagers, the telephone is the lifeline to most friendships and is a very comfortable tool.

The trick here is juggling a desire to have communication while monitoring costs. It is a reality that many families are not in the same geographical area and long distance charges come into the picture. Clear communication about what one can afford will diminish the chance for misunderstandings. When one family can afford more than the other, the relationship can be stressed. It is important that money not become a major focus. The family who can afford more needs to be especially sensitive. No one wants to feel inferior because of financial differences, and money frequently means status and power in our society. Those who have more power tend to have more control. The adoption experience is already loaded with control issues, and it is important not to let financial differences create even more power and control problems.

Sometimes, when long distance telephone charges get too high, the families make fewer calls in an effort to cut costs. When this happens, it can produce anxiety because there is a fear that all contact is about to stop. The concern is that it doesn't really have to do with the phone bill, but instead that one or the other party actually wants less contact. Being clear about the reason for calling less often will help everyone involved be less fearful of losing contact. Everyone benefits from bearing in mind that going into debt can seriously create conflicts in a family. The early stages are loaded enough with issues that involve juggling emotions, relationships, resources and time.

Eventually, all these areas tend to smooth out. The need and desire to talk constantly to one another eventually goes away as the relationship becomes more ongoing and predictable. In the early stages, adolescents have a need to be close to their birthparents and to get to know them. Sometimes, this need is met by a visit to the birthparent's home. This allows an up-close view of the birthparent.

Identity issues are important in all stages of development. Adolescence is particularly focused on the questions of "who am I?". Connecting with birthfamily provides the opportunity to get a clearer sense of self at this critical time. Grounding symbolizes security and rootedness. Finding relatives who have similar physical, emotional and intellectual attributes tends to help children feel grounded and helps them form a clearer sense of identity. Adopted persons of all ages are often amazed that there are others who actually share their characteristics.

Many adopted people also say they have a hard time feeling that they were born like everyone else, as though their lives began with the adoption rather than birth. When they make contact with their birthfamily and look into the eyes of their relatives, they have a feeling of being born and of being related to others through the generations. They often say that this makes them feel more whole. During adolescence, identity issues are being dealt with in a major way. Contacting his birthfamily allows the teenager to address these issues, resulting in a stronger sense of self as he enters adulthood.

It is important to say that none of this implies that adoptive parents and the adoptive family are not important. On the contrary, it is an acknowledgment that every adopted child has both a family of origin and a family by adoption. Each family has an important role in the life of the child. The love bonds between the adopted child and his adoptive parents are vital for the well-being of the child. Having access to all parts of oneself, by birth and adoption, is what is important for him.

Helping teens anticipate emotions, questions and situations can be very helpful with the voice of an experienced third party. During this stage, peers are so influential that these important issues may be better considered when heard from someone other than parents. This in no way discounts the importance of strong communication that may happen in a family. It just allows for the possibility of added resources as needed. Feelings for birthparents usually build, and a sense of disloyalty towards adoptive parents may accompany the expression of these. Being able to discuss these issues with someone not emotionally involved, but experienced with adoption issues, will help a young person understand that this is normal and also help them move through these feelings.

While not every opened adoption involves professionals who are guiding the way, everyone involved can benefit from their experience. Although opening an adoption may seem simple, once into it, it becomes clear that it is very complicated. When the goal is to increase positive outcomes, seeking knowledge and direction will be of benefit to all involved.

Books on search and reunion

Birthbond: Reunions Between Birthparents and Adoptees
by Judith Gediman and Linda Brown.

Birthright: The Guide to Search and Reunion for Adoptees,
Birthparents and Adoptive Parents
by Jean Strauss.

The Stranger Who Bore Me: Adoptee-Birth Mother Relationships
by Karen March.

Courageous Blessing - Adoptive Parents and The Search
by Carol Demuth.

Search Aftermath and Adjustments
by Pat Sanders & Nancy Sitterly.
(Can only be ordered through ISC Publications, P.O. Box 10192, Costa
Mesa, CA 92627. $8.00 per copy/includes shipping)

Sibling Reunions
by Randy Severson.

The Adoption Life Cycle
by Rosenburg.

Journey of the Adopted Self
by BJ Lifton.

Adoption Search: An Ethical Guide for Professionals
by Patricia Dorner.
(Available from Catholic Charities USA, 1731 King St., Suite 200,
Alexandria, VA 22314. 703-549-1390, x 38.)

Adoption organizations

Adoptees Liberty Movement Association, P.O. Box 154, Washington Bridge Station, New York, NY 10033. Phone: 212-581-1568.
Offers search and support for both birth parents and adoptees.

American Adoption Congress (AAC), 1000 Connecticut Ave., NW, Suite 9, Washington, DC 20036.
Advocates for adoption reform. Offers services to all members of the triad, including an annual conference, book catalog and newsletter.

Concerned United Birthparents (CUB), 2000 Walker St., Des Moines, IA 50317. 800-822-2777.
Offers search and support information. Works toward family preservation and adoption reform. Services includes various publications and a quarterly newsletter.

International Soundex Reunion Registry (ISRR), PO Box 2312, Carson City, NV 89702. 702-882-7755.
Links adoptees with birthparents and other family members.

Book catalogs

Heart Words Center, 4054 McKinney Ave., Suite 302, Dallas, TX 75204. 214-521-4560.
Books and tapes by Randy Severson.

R-Squared Press, 721 Hawthorne, Royal Oak, MI 48067. 810-543-0997.
Open Adoption Birthparent newsletter, Family Tree and books.

Tapestry, PO Box 359, Ringoes, NJ 08551-0359. 800-765-2367.
Full line of adoption related books

Chapter 7

Making Contact

Making the contact in a sensitive manner is of vital importance. It sets the tone for what follows. There are some variations on how to do this that seem to make a difference when contacting birthparents as opposed to adoptive parents. This seems to be true whether the contact is made by a professional or by the families themselves.

I have found that a birthmother (more about birthfathers later) can usually be safely approached by placing a discreet phone call. If a telephone number cannot be located, a cautiously written note could be sent. In the event that the call occurs at a time when she cannot speak freely, one is able to set a more convenient time. It is wise to ask yes/no questions in case there are others present during the call.

Mentioning the date of birth of the adopted child is one very effective way to let the birthmother know what the call is about. Sometimes the date of birth is not remembered correctly. This makes the birthmother feel terrible. Helping her understand that this is not unusual can ease her anguish. The birth and adoption represent a time of tremendous crisis and memory can be clouded in these situations. On top of that, a lot of medication was often used during deliveries that were expected to result in adoptions. This often created a fog that was hard to lift. It is hardly surprising, then, that the correct birthday may not be remembered.

I have found that writing adoptive parents seems to work better than telephone contact. A call tends to take them off balance and decrease the likelihood that they will consider contact. Those who feel violated by the change in the perceived "rules", (i.e. limited indirect or no contact), have a chance to begin to digest the significance of the approach. Even those unwilling to participate, or angered by the contact, are better able to take some time to absorb the intended message. If an intermediary is being used, it is a good idea for him to reassure the adoptive parents that the birthparent is approaching in friendship and does not wish to cause their family harm. Nor is she trying to disrupt the adoption. It is a good idea to also state that it is normal for birthparents to wonder about their children. Keeping the tone of the letter respectful and not demanding is important. After all, any form of contact will have to be with mutual consent.

A follow-up contact by phone, (indicated in the letter), would allow for further discussion of how contact can proceed. When some time passes between the letter and the follow up call there is a higher likelihood that a calmer conversation will take place. Sometimes adoptive parents will initiate the call themselves to react to the letter, so the letter should contain the appropriate telephone number.

Adoption related exchanges are so emotionally loaded, even with receptive parties, that information gets misheard, blocked out, or significantly turned around. This can put the desired outcome of contact at risk. Caution is indicated here because sometimes people feel pressured if they are contacted even more than once. Getting permission to write or call again can be a safeguard for everyone.

The role of geographical distance

The geographical distance between the adoptive family and the birthparent will often play a part in how the contact evolves. When the families live in the same town, there is a tendency to do less letter writing and call one another on the phone sooner. Many people feel that it is strange to be writing letters when they are so close to one another. It is sometimes tempting to rush into contact because it is so easy to get together. It is still a good idea to take into consideration that easing into the relationship benefits everyone, especially the children.

Living within easy reach of one another allows for a clearer picture of each other's lives. Living close by, however, does not guarantee frequent contact. Families are often short on time in our hectic society. Sometimes gatherings in families happen only for special occasions. What living within close range does offer is the opportunity for more frequent and spontaneous visiting. It increases the likelihood of getting together when travel costs are not a consideration.

On the other hand, for birthfamilies and adoptive families who live far away from each other, distance builds in a buffer to the intensity, especially at the early stages. Sometimes a more solid foundation is created because contact tends to be less overwhelming. It does take determination to develop a relationship when distance is a factor, but the payoff is that ties have a chance to develop gradually.

When both families live far away from one another, visits are usually longer than when the families live close by. This is because when travel is required, visits are not as frequent. In these cases, the maximum time recommended would be a weekend visit. Time together can be distributed over the two-day period. This reduces the intensity of the visit for everyone. Remember, these are emotionally-laden encounters and paying attention to this will help the relationship grow in manageable ways.

Distance also tends to feed fantasies about each other. It is quite normal to build a picture in one's mind about the other person based on what is being shared. We all tend to want to put our best foot forward. Included in this is the fact that all of us have a part of ourselves that we only share with our immediate family. Everyone makes decisions about what personal information is shared with others, be it family or friends. This will influence the fantasies and impressions others have about us.

Sometimes, when the worlds of adoptive and birthparents are very different, living some distance away from one another can be helpful. The reason for this is that the differences between them are not as obvious as if they lived in nearby communities. Letter writing and phone calls can put the two families on a more even footing than if they were seeing each other in person on a regular basis. I am talking here of people who might not otherwise cross paths had it not been for the child they share. Their values, beliefs, and behaviors may be very different and therefore could create stress and discomfort in the relationship. This does not mean that love and relationships can't be built when people are different. However, the reality is that relationships grow more easily when people have things in common.

Getting to know one another requires work as all sorts of facts and impressions about each other are assessed and absorbed. Intermittent visits require getting reacquainted over and over because of the time between visits. When dealing with young children this may be more obvious because even short time intervals feel huge. It is not unusual for adolescents to also exhibit anxiety even when visits have happened before. As with family and friends, as the years pass, the more contact there is, the more comfortable everyone becomes.

The complexity of this was demonstrated by a 15 year old on her way to visit her birthfamily for a few hours in another state, accompanied by her mother. Though contact happened frequently through letters and telephone calls, she hadn't seen her birthfamily for 3 years. On the way, she showed her nervousness by saying she really didn't want to go visit. She said it was all her mother's wish and not hers. Nonetheless, the two went on with the plans because the mother knew that the teen's anxiety was normal since she had not seen her birthfamily in a long time. They were able to talk about it and this helped the teen manage her emotions.

As expected, once everyone got together and the teen was able to relax, the visit was enjoyable. She later said she was so glad she had proceeded as planned. Several months later she said she wanted to visit her birthmother by herself for two weeks. While this may seem to be a dramatic shift, it is not unusual for this to happen as those involved get more comfortable with each other.

Geographical distance will influence how the relationship develops. It will affect the frequency and intensity of personal visits. Whether near or far, the families can make it work when everyone is committed to staying in touch.

More about visits

There are some additional points for birthparents and adoptive parents to think about as they plan the first visit. A good way to build cooperative bonds among the adults is to meet first without the adopted child. Time spent together in this way helps to build trust and allows them to plan the first visit in a mutually agreeable way. Teenagers may not be too pleased with this approach, but I have found it to be constructive in creating a foundation for a long-term relationship.

Also, think about who will participate in the first meeting with the child. Both adoptive parents should be there as support for their child and to show the child that they are comfortable with what is happening. Obviously, there will be times when only one parent can be present, especially if the cost of travel is a factor. In these cases, the parent who cannot attend is able to give his or her blessing and to discuss the visit afterwards. What is important is to let the child know that his parents are behind him through each step of the contact with the birthparent.

There are those who also wish to pay transportation costs for a visit. First visits don't seem to create a problem when funded this way.

As long as one party doesn't become the main source for picking up costs, the balance seems to be maintained. When one family is better off than the other, it is wise to not let money become too much of a focus. This tends to damage relationships. When it is possible to discuss these matters candidly, a better understanding occurs. The caution is not to make financial considerations a central focus. Observing appropriate protocol about money and its place in relationships is relevant here.

It is recommended that neither adoptive parents nor birthparents assume financial obligation for each other. There may be temptations to rescue or provide for each other, but time and time again this has interfered with the primary focus of building healthy, long term bonds.

A birthparent may choose to participate alone or include a spouse. The most important thing is not to overload the first meeting with a large number of people. While the birthparent may wish to include her children, it is wise to wait for future visits. First meetings are very intense and adding siblings to the picture makes them even more complicated.

Adopted children are usually eager to meet the birthsiblings. Even so, it is best to do things gradually. It is truly a gift when children separated by adoption are able to build sibling bonds through contact at an early age because getting to know one another takes time and effort. This is especially true because the children live in different households and frequently in different towns.

Another set of siblings to consider are the ones in the adoptive family. They too benefit from being included in this important family venture. Whenever possible, it is a good idea to include them after the first visit. They too have a great deal to digest as contact is being established.

As all the children get to know one another, sibling rivalries may occur. This is normal in blended families. The children also tend to claim each other as brothers and sisters in a way that has to do with kinship ties that are not always created by blood.

The building relationship benefits from the thoughtful planning of the birthparents and the adoptive parents. By the time a visit is arranged, the two sets of parents have already cooperated quite a bit. The extent to which their friendship develops depends on the same factors which govern other meaningful relationships outside of adoption.

When contact is not possible

There will be times when contact is not possible. The most typical scenarios involve adoptive parents who are fearful of the birthparents' entry in their lives or who believe it would be detrimental to their child. Birthparents who do not participate often cite that their children and/or spouses do not know about the adopted child. They are not willing to risk losing these relationships especially after already experiencing the loss of the adopted child. They also express a grief so intense, that allowing the opening of the often suppressed wounds, is more than they can bear.

The beauty of the invitational approach is that a door is opened that was previously shut. Adoptive parents learn that the birthparent(s) care and are open to contact. They can no longer hide behind the beliefs of the past about birthparents not caring or not wishing to be found.

Even when birthparents can't participate, they learn that the adoptive family values their involvement and that the child benefits from their participation. Where before they might not have considered their role to be significant, now they begin to understand that they are very important.

Through the years, there have been many who returned later, seeking contact due to the knowledge brought about by the original invitation. The change of heart often is guided by acknowledged needs as well as a desire to respond to the needs of others. Looking at it this way, there is never a failed contact. A door of new awareness and future possibility is always opened.

Writing an introductory letter - considerations for birthparents and adoptive parents

Both birthparents and adoptive parents need to:
- Keep the tone respectful. Address anticipated fears and concerns.
- Convey why you wish to open the adoption at this time - this builds understanding.
- Provide information about your life—help them get a sense of who you are.
- Provide them with an address or telephone number so you can be contacted.
- Emphasize you do not wish to rush into anything and will respect boundaries.
- Show an understanding of the differences between a birthparent's role and an adoptive parents role in an open adoption.
- Briefly describe the benefits you see in opening up the adoption.
- Allow time for the request to be considered but give them suggestions for possible next steps.

Writing to children - considerations for birthparents

- Keep it simple.
- Let the child know you love him and have thought about him through the years.
- Tell him briefly about your life: whether you are married; have other children, their ages and names; what you like to do (hobbies and talents); favorite foods, music, colors, etc.; if you have pets.
- "Listen" to your child's letters. What is he asking about? What is he interested in?
- Ask him questions about his life.
- Include a picture of yourself.
- Keep the content age appropriate. Save details of the adoption story for later.
- Speak well of his parents-this is a team effort.

Talking on the phone

1. The first contact between birthparents and adoptive parents.
   - Being nervous is normal—remember you are still getting acquainted.
   - Think about language. How do you refer to each other and to the adopted child?
   - Prepare a list of questions to ask and information to share.
   - Everyone has the right to share what is comfortable and to withhold what is not. Respecting each other's privacy is important.
   - Discuss the next step. Some may want to keep it open ended, others may want to set another date and time.

2. The first contact between birthparents and the adopted child.
   - Write questions and information to share. This helps to make the conversation more comfortable.
   - It is recommended that the adults greet each other first. This helps the child see the relationship between their birthparent and their adoptive parents.
   - This is a family connection therefore, the adoptive parents serve as the facilitators for the call. They may stay on the line if the child requests this, if the child is quite young or if there is a reason to monitor the call.
   - If a professional is involved, he will usually stay on the line during the first call to assist the child. Afterwards, he can help the child process how the call went.
   - Let the child guide how long they wish to speak.

Chapter 8

The Role of Commitment

Adult commitment is a very important ingredient in the process of reconnection. All parties are emotionally vulnerable. For this reason, birthparents and adoptive parents need to consciously commit to nurture the relationship over time. Children should not be responsible for sustaining relationships with adults. Therefore, adoptive parents and birthparents must explore this area as it requires mutual dedication. It is they who devote the time and effort to keep the door open. It is essential to only agree to do what is comfortable for all concerned. Where closed adoptions prohibit relationships, open adoption is built on them.

Birthparents express a fear that once they participate, events may cut them off one more time. The emotional risk can be mammoth. Sometimes children are satisfied with a brief exchange. Don't force children to participate when they don't wish to. It is important, though, to leave the door open so they can do so later on when they again feel ready to have contact. It is the adoptive parent's responsibility to not drop the birthparent because the child appears to be satisfied for the moment. This means that they will continue to update the birthfamily on how the child is doing, developing an adult initiated exchange.

Birthparents have responsibilities as well. Their continued participation is also important even when the child has a decreased interest in contact. This allows the child to see that the birthparent is not going to disappear on him again. It does take a great deal of emotional energy to continue communication with a non responsive child. However, even when there is not much acknowledgment from the child, he is paying attention to the continuing efforts. If the child's emotional needs are kept as the main focus, then adults are better able to forgo some of their needs. This is not intended to hurt birth or adoptive parents. Rather, the effort here is to bring out that during this very complicated journey, the adults are making substantial efforts to stay child centered.

One meaningful way to remain visible to the child is to celebrate birthdays and holidays with cards and/or gifts. Being remembered at these significant times is very important for children. It also permits the birthparents to do something positive. Even when the desire is to do more, there is mutual benefit derived from at least this much.

When adoptions are opened, family members who were not acknowledged before are now invited into the family fold. With time, the two families will become clearer about the developing ties. It is quite usual to see other relatives join the picture, expanding the extended family concept. As moments are shared, there will be an ongoing definition of the roles that family members will have.

The avenues for contact are the same as in other friendship and family connections. Therefore, there may be letter and picture exchanges, telephone calls and visits in person. The frequency of these will be guided by both families. Building a pattern of respectful contact takes time as the families by birth and adoption get to know each other and learn how each handles a variety of situations.

There tends to be a caution in families by adoption that is not quite as evident in other family structures. This has to do with the fear of overstepping and jeopardizing the contact. While it is advisable to be respectful of others, allowing for extra sets of siblings, grandparents, aunts and uncles is a reality in open adoptions. Each is a relative and a potential relationship.

In the beginning, it will be important to discuss roles, degrees of involvement and titles to be used. In looking at families joined by marriage, there are givens about the roles people will fill and where they belong within the family. For example, when children are born, the parents of the husband and wife become the grandparents. This is quite well-defined in our society. Each family has its own rituals and rules that allow for the interweaving of the resulting relationships. When adoptions are opened, family relationships also have to be defined. For example, here too, the role of grandparents belongs to the parents of the adoptive parents and to the parents of the birthparents.

While this seems obvious, there is sometimes resistance to allowing these family relationships to be called by there proper names. This has to do with the difficulty that some people have with sharing the children. This interferes with making the most of the connection that open adoption offers. As families joined by adoption figure out their relationships, their kinship ties will be defined more clearly, contributing to their sense of commitment to one another. Commitment is the necessary backbone for continuous relationships.

When all isn't equal among adopted siblings

Adoptive parents often express concern about opening the adoption for one of their children when it might be impossible for the other. There is no question that it can be very painful for a child to be left out of the reconnection process. Some of this is eased by at least making visible efforts to reach out to the other child's birthfamily and expressing empathy to the affected child. While the timing for both families to participate may not be the same, at least the door is opened. While this does not take away the child's hurt, he does tend to feel closer to his adoptive parents because they have shown an understanding of his needs. Feeling supported and understood helps children feel connected to, and loved by, their parents.

In truth, there are many situations that present themselves where all is not equal for our children from the anguish of being excluded from a birthday party to not making a team. Each family develops strategies for coping. Some of the ways to do this will be to keep adoption communication open. This does not mean talking about adoption everyday, but it does mean creating an atmosphere where parents and children may talk about adoption freely.

Additionally, when opening an adoption, birthfamilies and adoptive families become extended family to one another. It follows that birthrelatives are the relatives of all the other adopted children. This allows the children the vicarious benefit of experiencing birthfamily. Each family becomes a support and a resource for the other.

Involving the whole family through this process is one way to accomplish the inclusion of the child who doesn't have a birthfamily connection. He may be invited to write or send a picture. When meeting, he too can participate. This is a family function, after all. There is sometimes a heightened sense of vulnerability in these siblings that somehow the birthfamily will take away his sibling. By claiming a sibling's birthfamily, the sense of risk is lessened. Speaking openly about this will put these concerns out in the open. It is also helpful to discuss the situation with members of the birthfamily so they can be sensitive to the child. Most families are eager to be helpful to all the children in the adoptive family.

This was so beautifully demonstrated in a family where the 17 year old had had contact with her birthmother from a very young age. Due to major struggles on the part of the birthmother, silence had been her response to several letters at critical times in this child's life. The child needed to hear from the birthmother and was deeply hurt. To cope with the hurt, she reached out to the person she considered another mother figure, her sister's birthmother. In this way, she received some of what she needed from her own birthmother: attention, acknowledgment, and love. Just the fact that it was a birthmother who was doing this was meaningful to the child and helped her cope.

Families often have significant people in their lives who are emotionally supportive. This then, is an example of a birthfamily being a meaningful resource to the adoptive family.

The role and significance of gift-giving

The desire to give gifts when adoptions are opened is very typical. After all, uncelebrated birthdays and Christmases have passed year after year. The opportunity to finally celebrate these important events, may unleash an unrestrained desire to bestow a mountain of gifts. Caution is well served here as an unending flow may create problems.

While children love receiving gifts, an overabundance from birthparents often gets interpreted as "he's trying to buy my love." This becomes counterproductive in an already very delicate dance. It is suggested that when a gift is given, especially at the early stages, that it be one that does not go overboard in cost. We realize that this is relative in every family, where financial capabilities differ. One might take into consideration realistic personal finances as well as the capabilities of the receiving family.

We have seen stuffed animals be gifts of choice in many situations. Having missed the chance to give presents through the years, meets a need within. Children of all ages love these. Mike received a teddy bear the first time his parents met with his birthmother. When he saw her, she brought pictures which were a perfect choice. There was discussion about future gifts funded jointly by the birthmother and the adoptive parents because Mike tended to destroy his belongings when he was upset. By joining in gift giving, perhaps he would not be so conflicted about gifts from either party. This creative idea came from his adoptive parents.

Some birthparents make the first gift very special, such as a piece of jewelry and then let gift giving happen at appropriate times such as birthdays and Christmas. This balance seems to work well.

Reopening open adoptions

When open adoptions occur, both the adoptive parents and the birth parents who are involved share identities with one another. This includes names, addresses, and phone numbers. In this way, staying in touch directly with one another is made possible and very straightforward. The assumption is that, in the planning of the adoption, all parties have begun to build a relationship with one another and that they will want to stay in touch through the years. This, after all, is what guides the open adoption practice: a blended family is created and everyone has the opportunity to benefit as in extended families. However, we have observed that there are situations where contact is lost for a variety of reasons. These even include those for whom friendship seemed to be a significant ingredient for a lengthy period of time. What happened?

One scenario that we see involves people who agreed to an open adoption so that there would be an adoption. In these situations, very little takes place once the adoption occurs. When it is the adoptive parents who withdraw, it seems that the main reason has to do with a possessiveness of the child mixed with a fear of the birthmother. The desire to be the "only parents" to the child is usually present. This behavior is often justified by our society where an understanding of adoption is limited at best, and usually, misguided. The message often is: "After all, what rights do birthparents have? They signed their rights away! Why would you want to stay in touch?"

A birthparent faced with these situations finds herself in shock, feeling betrayed by the people to whom she entrusted her child. She begins to examine what effect this might have not only on herself, but on the adopted child. She begins to question how the adoptive parents will be able to handle the topic of adoption in a positive manner. She is also concerned what kind of messages will be given about the birthparents and why the adoption took place. Being available to participate in the child's life but blocked from doing so, the birthparent worries that the child will experience abandonment and rejection issues so typical in adopted persons. In the absence of legally binding agreements, one's word is the essence of these adoptions. Rebuilding trust then, becomes the focal point when contact is being reestablished.

It is wise to keep the door open by maintaining contact in whatever form is possible. Frightened people sometimes need evidence that their fears are unfounded. Communicating a commitment to the relationship may be one option. Fear of birthparents is typical in our society. Even when people have known each other face to face, there is a vulnerability to being swayed by the larger community regarding this fear.

Efforts to reestablish a relationship may go through many stages from gentle to intense. One way for birthparents to document the continued desire to stay in touch is by sending birthday and Christmas greetings. It is a good idea to keep copies of correspondence so as to keep a record of one's efforts.

When a birthparent is the one who phases herself out after the adoption, it is often related to the grief of separating from her child and dealing with a new role and status in the child's life. To go from the total caregiver, while the child is in utero, to being a birthparent is very painful, and for some, unbearable. Separating herself from the adoptive family becomes a self protective effort in the hopes of making the pain more manageable. What she often doesn't realize is that buried and unaddressed grief often shows itself in other forms. This may show up as general depression, difficulty in establishing close relationships, physical problems, and in other ways.

Sometimes a birthparent is so pleased with her choice of adoptive parents, that she feels she is no longer important in the child's life. She diminishes herself to such a degree, that fading out is the outcome. The education and counseling before the adoption even takes place is very crucial in emphasizing that both sets of parents are important for this child and that both sets have a responsibility to sustain the relationship. Using the blended family concept is helpful in teaching this. Most people know families where the children are his, hers, and ours. The children deal with all sorts of relatives. Usually, there is encouragement for the various family members to stay in the picture. Having support available, when questions and issues arise, is essential. This does not mean that families continuously need therapists in their lives. Rather, supports are there as one walks through challenging or scary stages of life.

Adoptive parents who counted on an open adoption express disappointment when the birthparent of their child fades out. They also worry about how this will affect their child over time. These parents know the benefits of a cooperative relationship with birthparents. That is why they opted for an open adoption in the first place. Continuing to invite the birthparent into the relationship is one avenue to keeping the door open. Just the fact that adoptive parents understand why birthparents disengage will be helpful for all concerned. We see a lot of empathy for the birthparent's dilemma and less of a judgmental position on the part of the adoptive parents. This makes it easier for the birthparents to participate again at some other time when they can better handle it.

Life events also play a part in stopping the contact between adoptive and birthfamilies. Sometimes even long standing relationships are discontinued because of life stages involving education, marriage, jobs, and growing families. In our mobile society, the parting of ways may relate to geographical distance, where it takes more work to stay in touch.

There are also those who lose sight of why the connection happened in the first place and what the issues are that make staying connected important. Additionally, friends, family members or new mates may question the value or good judgment of this practice. An environment not supportive of these ties, may have the power to sever them. People start feeling insecure about whether they are doing the right thing. Support groups and continued contact with others in the open adoption journey can give these folks the encouragement they need to stay involved.

The advantage these individuals have when trying to reestablish a relationship after some time has passed, is that they have each other's identity. This is a major head start in reconnecting with one another. This is very different from a closed adoption where time, energy, and funds are usually spent in just locating the identity of the other party.

As a result of what has been discussed so far, there are families who make serious efforts to reopen their adoptions. Contact has been broken off and is now being sought again after a time period of silence. When the birthparent continues to be unwilling to respond, yet another concern arises. The children, who are now older, are absorbing the silence and usually interpreting it as rejection. There comes a point when the hurt is so great that efforts to get in touch stop. The children's message may be, "I am not interested any more." In fact, this is a self protective device to avoid further hurt. Emphasizing that the birthparent is struggling with her own issues is important. Children feel rejected yet one more time when the invitation to know them is turned down.

In these situations pain is unavoidable, but work can be done to help the children not blame themselves. Acknowledging whatever feelings they identify, will be important here. Sometimes a letter from the child and the adoptive parents to the birthparent helps the birthparent understand his needs. This will sometimes pave the way for further contact.

In a similar manner, there are birthparents who wish to renew the contact but who meet resistance. This is very painful and, as a result, they tend to retreat waiting for the child to become an adult when an approach could reoccur. Efforts to build understanding about one's needs, whether the birthparents' or the adoptive family's, sometimes prove fruitless. The fact is that sometimes there will not be a response or a willingness to stay in touch.

We have said that open adoption involves maintaining bonds as defined by the participants. So, technically, the adoption once opened is always open even during periods of no contact. Still, there is work needed to cross paths again establishing a current understanding about and with each other no matter how much time has passed.

Many of the topics previously discussed throughout this book will also apply to those who want to reopen their adoptions. Depending on those involved, it may be possible to establish a comfortable relationship with ease just as we do with old friends that we see only occasionally. The advantage is that these people are stepping into situations that are already more familiar than those involving closed adoptions. The fear and risk factors tend to be lower, but in many ways similar to those in closed adoptions wanting to open them.

It is wise to try to connect directly with the person one is seeking and to respect his or her privacy. While no one can force someone to participate, updating the message of the open door is a gift. Too often assumptions are made as to why there has been no contact. Rather than spending a lot of energy guessing, efforts to build something mutually comfortable would be encouraged.

Sometimes all it may take is a phone call or a letter to the desired person. When that approach does not succeed because of changed names and addresses, one may have to pursue a search. Adoption professionals and search groups are often used in these situations. An intermediary is typically not needed here since there have been pre-existing bonds. If one wishes to use an experienced facilitator, it might offer a chance to do some groundwork so the whole cycle doesn't keep repeating itself.

How can these situations that cause so much anguish be minimized? A beginning point is for all to learn as much as possible about the different faces and stages of adoption before the adoption even happens. While it is impossible to anticipate every angle, a good preparation allows for a more realistic view of the adoption journey. As in many life situations, having an awareness of what may come up provides helpful checkpoints.

Similarities and differences between the search and the opening of closed adoptions

Adoption core issues for triad members are the same whether one has an open or closed adoption. I am speaking here of issues such as grief, loss, rejection, abandonment and shame. Closed adoption offers few avenues for knowledge of the truth behind the adoption.

Communication is often limited even when there is a willingness to have dialogue within the adoptive family. Filling in the gaps often depends on a search for birth relatives since records are sealed in most states. The amount of energy, money and time that are needed to accomplish one's goal tends to be substantial. The drive to complete a search is personally timed. Searching is often delayed because both adoptees and birthparents fear rejection By the time one pursues this quest, adoption issues have been identified as troubling and needing action.

Open adoption brings the issues out into the open and offers an opportunity to work on them with the significant parties: the adopted person and his adoptive and birth parents. The handling of these issues will be determined by the individual's developmental stages.

For example, a four- or five-year-old will wonder if he grew inside his mommy. It helps him understand that he grew inside someone else when that person is real to him. Knowing the birthmother in person helps the child begin to take in that he grew within her and is now with the mommy who is raising him. In fact, he has a mommy he lives with and a birthmommy who gave him life. Since young children have a hard time with abstract concepts, the open adoption experience allows the birthparent to be a real person instead of an abstract one.

Another situation might involve a school-age child who is angry about his adoption. The birthparent is able to tell him directly why the adoption happened and how much she continues to love him. The child benefits from hearing from his birthmother directly. In some cases, it is the birthfather who is the one who talks with the child about whatever is on his mind.

By being able to keep in contact, adoption is addressed, as needed, over time. When addressed openly, the possibility for healing is greater. The younger the child is when this can happen, the earlier the emotional work can occur. This is not a cure all, one time event. Rather, the emotional work takes place over the years, examined and re-examined as needed. The beauty of involving children is that needs can be tended to as they arise, rather than putting them off to adulthood. Every year that passes makes the questions more intense.

As the needs of the child get met, there tends to be increased bonding with family and others and a sense of self that is clearer through access to birthparents. Also, instead of using a lot of energy to wonder about his adoption, the child can use his energy elsewhere. The strengthening that happens with the connection can begin during the childhood years instead of being delayed to adulthood. Adoptive parents and birthparents are able to participate actively and cooperatively. This allows them to also work on the issues pertaining to them.

In the case of minor children, the adults are the ones who guide the exchanges. Adoptive parents evaluate what they feel is appropriate for their child. Birthparents participate in a manner that becomes mutually comfortable. Adult searchers and their birthparents guide their own reconnection process. Adoptive parents usually participate at the invitation of their adult children. Sometimes adopted adults are not given full adult status by their birthparents or society. It is appropriate that they, as adults, determine who participates as they reconnect with the birthfamily. Unfortunately, there are states where the ability to search requires adoptive parent endorsement no matter what the age of the adult. This demonstrates to what lengths society is capable of going to maintain a childhood status for adopted adults.

When working with minors, I have suggested a gradual pacing leading up to physical contact. This allows the children time to process and absorb everything that is going on within and around them. Adopted adults who have contacted the birthfamily also benefit from taking their time to get acquainted. However, it is quite usual for them to enter into direct contact very quickly. As adults, they have the right to make decisions about each step they take. Being older and more mature, they are in a better place to make adjustments along the way if the contact moves too fast for them or the birthparents.

The working out of adoption issues is a lifetime process. The younger the person, the greater the opportunity to sort out whatever needs emotional attention. Even if gradual resolution occurs over time, at least there is the possibility to integrate one's truth at an earlier age, thus shedding baggage that can follow well into adulthood.

Both adults and children feel more whole and more grounded through contact with the birthfamily. The search is a delayed response to a need that we understand is normal. Through the opening of adoptions the need is addressed in a much earlier manner whereby all parties benefit.

Chapter 9

Opening Adoptions of Special Needs Children

In discussing special needs children, I am focusing particularly on those who were removed from the care of their birthparents, usually involuntarily. Included in this group are those children who have experienced abuse and neglect. They have typically been through the foster care system with multiple placements. They face the same issues as other adopted children plus a significant number of additional and complex ones. Physical and emotional wounds are so deep that efforts to heal through family work is vital.

It is not unusual for all contact with the birthfamily to be discontinued when an adoption occurs. Even when the placing agent may allow some level of contact, there is often none. Once the adoption is finalized, the decision making is in the hands of the adoptive parents. Knowing the child's history and feeling his pain, adoptive parents sometimes are opposed to allowing birthfamily members in. Many adoptive parents feel tremendous anger towards birthparents who have emotionally or physically hurt their children. They are also often fearful that the children may suffer again at the hands of birthparents . Especially when these birthparents were opposed to the adoption. There can also be a fear that the child might get kidnapped. Sometimes this is a valid concern.

While these situations are complicated and need special consideration, the opening of these adoptions can be of great value. These children also need to know the truth about why they were adopted. Communication with the birthfamily is an important avenue for obtaining this knowledge. The birthparents were often the ones who abused or neglected the children. In spite of this, the children often express a desire to somehow have them in their lives. This requires evaluation of the ability of everyone concerned to manage the ensuing relationships.

Sometimes birth siblings and extended birthfamily members are involved as a first step. It is not unusual, while children are in foster care, for visits to take place with various family members. To suddenly stop these when an adoption occurs, is not in keeping with what adoption professionals believe to be healthy. Nonetheless, it happens.

Adoptions with older children are very complicated. It is, therefore, wise to use an experienced third party. By handling it this way, an assessment of the adoptive and birthfamily situation can lead to sound recommendations.

Foster parents who adopt seem to have a greater sense of comfort with keeping up birth family connections. They are used to birthfamily involvement as part of the foster care model. When an adoption happens, roles are changed. Being able to switch from temporary caretaker to permanent parent is an important step. Before, the system made major decisions for the child, but now the adoptive parents take on that role.

Having had experience with the birth relatives of the child, they are in an excellent position to evaluate what type of contact may be possible and sound. They will take into account the needs and strengths of the child. The child's therapist can help as well, if the child is in therapy, which is often the case. The team effort is valuable when making decisions on behalf of these children.

Birthparents being invited into their children's lives have to accept their changed role. This can be difficult because they have had a parenting role at one time. For better or worse, they also have had shared memories. Most of these birthparents have had serious problems and don't have sound parenting skills. They too, have often been part of the foster care system, abused and neglected by their parents. In their own way, they have loved their children even as they have hurt them. The empathy and understanding of adoptive parents sometimes allows them to be forgiving of these birthparents. When this happens, they are better able to open the door to contact while being protective of the children's welfare.

Special needs children carry with them confused as well as accurate memories. Speaking with birth relatives allows them to sort out their history. While remembering can be very painful, bringing feelings out into the open can allow for healing. Birthparents are able to assume responsibility for their mistakes and help the child move on. I have seen even very troubled birthparents do this with a sincerity that makes a difference.

The preparation of the birthfamily is, therefore, very important. Helping them understand that they can do something sound for their child, will be of benefit to that birthparent and the child. When birthparents are not treated as vile human beings, they are better able to rise to the occasion and do what is right for their child.

The child needs to know that, even though this birthparent is not able to properly raise him, there is still caring in her heart. Hand in hand with this is the importance of giving the child permission to belong in and love his adoptive family. When both sets of parents tell the child that loving the other is O.K., the child is freed to be a part of both families.

It is indeed remarkable to see how the loving hearts of adoptive parents open the door to birthparents who may still be in jail, still involved with drugs, or other life situations that present risk. Getting beyond their own needs, they respond to their children.

James' (not his real name) adoptive parents raised him from birth. He had been born drug addicted and eventually was diagnosed as schizophrenic. When he was 17, they sought out his birthmother. They found her in jail. As the involved professional, I visited her and shared news about her child. Though her life was still in chaos, she was open to participating in whatever way was possible. She posed for a picture so that her son could see what she looked like.

As part of the preparation for all, the adoptive mother went to visit her at the jail. Willing to take whatever steps were necessary, she conveyed an acceptance of this birthmother's life. At some point later in time, when the birthmother was released from jail, this family invited her into their home so that they all could get acquainted. They had evaluated that there was not a danger in doing this. Instead, the benefits outweighed the risks.

This family opened the adoption further by including other birth relatives and a brother who had been adopted by another family. With their eyes open, they allowed their son's birth family into their lives guided by the understanding that this was important for him. James benefited from knowing about his roots. He expressed a satisfaction with seeing people who looked like he did and shared other characteristics as well. Being an Hispanic in an Anglo family, he felt a greater peace about being different from his adoptive parents. He developed a stronger sense of identity and belonging. Before this, he had been unable to truly feel the acceptance and love of his adoptive parents. Now, he even saw their acceptance of his still troubled birthmother. This translated to a clearer acceptance of him, no matter what existed in his birthfamily. He continued to be schizophrenic and to have more hospitalizations, but something had changed dramatically within him.

Andrea, 14 years old, had been part of her adoptive family for a few years. There had been continued contact with a sister. Andrea's emotional problems required hospitalizations. During one of these hospitalizations, her psychiatrist felt it was important for her to have contact with her birthparents. She had many fantasies about returning to her birthfamily. Her birthmother was not emotionally stable and was still totally opposed to the adoption. Other family members supported the need for the adoption.

The adoptive parents had to decide what kind of contact would be possible. They chose supervised visits. Planning meetings were held with the adoptive parents. A joint meeting with the birthparents and 6 birthsiblings followed. Andrea's problems and needs were described to her family. A plea was made for them to give her the go-ahead to move on with her life. It was also important for her to know they all cared about her even though she could not live with them.

The birthmother firmly stood her ground about how she had been wronged in losing her child. However, the power of the group, her own children, refocused her, and clearly told her she was wrong. When the meeting included Andrea, she was able to be part of the healing message, "we care about you and want you to go on with your life."

Jimmy, 12 years old, had been with his foster/ adoptive parents for about 7 years. He had not seen his birthmother for 4 years. Contact had been continuously maintained with his 2 older brothers (also adopted), his birthgrandparents, aunts and cousins. There was a great deal of trust with these family members to the extent that he even spent the night with them. The adoptive parents laid out ground rules regarding the birthmother, who had a history of drug addiction, had been imprisoned, and now was free.

It was decided that Jimmy needed to include his birthmother in his life again. She was now out of jail and was working on her life. She already had a track record, seeing her other two sons and behaving appropriately with them. This was taken into account, as planning began for a visit.

Jimmy's birthmother first met with me as the facilitator, so that an evaluation could occur. This was followed by a meeting with the adoptive parents. Prior to this, a few letters had been exchanged to get the communication going. Letter writing is one way to get reacquainted. It was felt that the next step could include Jimmy.

His parents and therapist did some beginning preparation with him. It was explained that the visit would hopefully be the first of many. No promises were made about how often these would be. He was told that, after the visit, he would leave with his parents. They scheduled a visit to his brothers' immediately afterwards so that he had something to look forward to after the parting with his birthmother.

The visit took place at a familiar McDonald's so that Jimmy could move about or play if he chose to. The planning included going to a nearby school yard with a basketball if the McDonald's didn't work out. This wasn't necessary. The visit lasted about 1 1/2 hours.. The conversation included current news and some talk about events of the past that were foggy to Jimmy. There were tears and laughter. His birthmom was able to tell him that she wanted him to do well with his adoptive parents and that she hoped to remain a part of his life.

Afterwards, Jimmy's therapist suggested that visits be scheduled on a regular basis so that he knew that he would see his birthmother in a predictable way. Caution would be exercised because, in the past, she had often disappointed her children by not showing up. Taking into account her ability to come through would be important.

These families, birth and adoptive, are ones that are willing to put themselves out to help their children work out their life journeys. Each has its own complicated features that must be taken into account. The fact that families are willing to take this walk is a statement about the importance of family ties even with horrendous histories of abuse and neglect. Every birthfamily has at least one person who can give a helping hand to these hurting children. For adoptive parents, finding a way to include meaningful people takes a deep belief that it is beneficial to their children to at least try.

What is The North American Council on Adoptable Children (NACAC)?

NACAC is an agency serving other agencies and organizations that place adoptable children; it isn't a child placement organization. NACAC mainly aids agencies place older and special needs children. It supports 600 adoptive parent groups across the United States and Canada and hosts an annual adoption and training conference.

Membership is encouraged for anyone interested in adoption issues and costs $40 a year. Members include parents, advocates, professionals, and policy makers. They receive discounts on conference fees and the quarterly newsletter, Adoptalk, which features adoption policies updates, individual family stories, articles written by experts, and other resources. NACAC also provides a list of research and special publications. NACAC can put anyone interested in adopting a child in touch with an agency or a parent group in their area.

For more information contact: 970 Raymond Ave., Suite 106, St. Paul, MN 55114-1149, Telephone: (612) 644-3036, Fax: (612) 644-9848, E-mail: NACAC@aol.com

Chapter 10

The Now Blended Family

I have spoken throughout this book about the blended family concept. As the years pass, it becomes clearer which family members stay connected across adoptive and birth family trees. Every family has varying degrees of communication among its members. Being able to rejoin whenever one wishes to is part of the benefit of having easy access to one another.

With time, the composition of both families will go through changes including births, deaths, marriages, divorces, and remarriages. This is normal in every family because life is fluid. Over time, there will be periods of relative calm and periods when family members may not get along. Realizing that this is normal helps families cope. Not putting adoption into its own different box helps people deal with each other from a point of reference that is familiar.

A birthmother whose daughter refused to see her during a visit to the child's home was hurt and disappointed. There had been no way to predict this child's behavior. The birthmother's husband, hurting for his wife, said, "I thought open adoption was supposed to be so much better." He seemed to believe that smooth times would be constant. There is no life experience that offers that.

As children integrate their two families, they absorb the different parts that make up their identity. A birthmother who had had an on-going open adoption with the family of her 15-year-old son, reflected on her diminished participation. She had been less in touch because life was hectic. Now her son was using her maiden name hyphenated with his adoptive last name. This troubled her as it felt wrong to her that he would do that. She felt it was disrespectful to his adoptive family.

We explored what this meant to all three parties. She imagined, knowing the open heart of the adoptive parents, that they would not be troubled in the least. Dare she be glad that her son claimed her by including her name? She realized that it was a conflict within herself of entitlement—the right to be acknowledged to that degree.

We discussed that names have tremendous significance, especially for an adopted person. Her son was in fact, showing a comfort with who he was through both his families. He was actively claiming both. She was able to understand that, in fact, this was healthy and that both sets of parents had paved the way for this through their continued joint efforts. As she realized that she was more important in his life than she had recently allowed, she committed to maintaining more on-going contact.

Sometimes children feel jealous of how adults develop their relationships. One teenager, who had been in touch with birthrelatives for most of her life, observed that her mom chatted on the phone for long periods of time with her birthmom. The two adults had developed a comfortable relationship. This child stayed on the phone for just a few minutes by choice. In her mind, the birthrelatives loved her mom more than her. Her birthrelatives were able to address this misconception and she moved on.

It is possible to describe an endless number of situations that arise as the two families interrelate through the years. The fact is, we are talking about relationships that are complex by nature. Perfect answers and solutions are not always available. We are best guided by good sense and seeking outside help in figuring out what to do when we are not sure.

Dealing with the community at large

Adoption has gone through so many changes in recent years that sometimes it is difficult for uninvolved people to understand how it works. Adoptive and birth families have an opportunity to educate their communities through the sharing of experiences.

. This sharing can happen in natural and comfortable ways. Those involved need to decide for themselves what they feel comfortable in discussing. They also need to be aware of how the other people involved may feel about what is being shared. Sometimes curious people ask questions that border on inappropriate. It is not necessary to answer except to the degree one wishes. Children are often exposed to the ignorant statements and it is the job of the adults in their lives to model what is desirable and sensible.

When birth and adoptive families have a relationship, unbelieving people may question the sanity of this. They may also ask probing questions as to why the adoption happened and for details that are not their business. Families have a right to respond that this information is personal and not discussed outside of the family. If there is a desire to share, then it should be with an awareness of its impact, especially on the children.

One typical school assignment is the family tree. Children are able to share whatever they wish. Often, their classmates and even their teachers may be perplexed by family trees including birth and adoptive families. Preparing children for these and other situations is a good idea.

A teenager chatting with a new friend, told him that she was adopted. First of all, he didn't believe her. She couldn't understand why it was not credible. The fact is, that the lack of belief is often connected to a negative feeling about adoption. As though the adopted girl should have been spared that label. His amazement continued when she told him that she had known her birthmother for many years. He wanted to know what she called her "real" mother. She told him that both her mothers were her real mothers. Incredulous still, he wanted to know how her adoptive mother felt about her feeling this way. When she told him that the two mothers were best friends, he was awed.

This young man learned many lessons about adoption that day. He was able to see that the girl was comfortable with what she was saying. With no defensiveness, she patiently explained whatever he didn't understand. This child had had extensive practice and felt at peace about her life. Not all children manage it in this way, but providing some help in anticipating these situations will make it easier to deal with whatever arises.

There will be a never ending number of opportunities to educate the community at large. This can be done through informal discussions and more structured methods. The latter may include the use of the media, school curricula, conferences, etc. As interested parties, it is up to those who make up the birth and adoptive families to make this part of their mission. The more understanding that is put out there for general use, the more support there will be for these families.

Impact on adoption practice—our role as advocates

The voices of those involved with adoption have had the power to create dramatic change in the practice of adoption. We have gone all the way from being completely secretive and disconnected to totally honest and rejoined. The depth of understanding about this complicated journey has grown in many directions. There are geographical regions where opened adoptions are quite commonplace. There are also areas where the resistance is as strong as the resistance to open records. This may be understandable because open adoption, in many ways, is equivalent to open records in that the identities are known by those who are involved.

It is crucial that families and professionals committed to open adoption join ranks to spread the word that it can work. Life doesn't promise a smooth sail to anyone. Therefore, open adoption doesn't have to be perfect. It just has to be honest and truthful. Families strive to do the best they can. When there are troubled times, they work on resolving problems. Sometimes they enlist the help of professionals to get them through. This after all, is the real world. Kinship ties are important. The opening of adoptions acknowledges this.